For my beloved
brother Brian on his
journey March 2004

. . . A ROMANCE FOR MEN GOING HOME

BOUND FOR THE

CRAGS OF ITHAKA

A Romance for Men Going Home

STEVEN FOSTER

LOST BORDERS PRESS
Big Pine, California

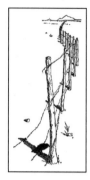

Lost Borders Press
P.O. Box 55
Big Pine, CA 93513
e-mail: lostbrdrs@telis.org
www.schooloflostborders.com

Library of Congress Cataloging-in-Publication Data

Foster, Steven, 1938–2003

Bound for the crags of ithaka: a romance for men going home

cm.

ISBN 0-9667659-3-1 $24.75

1. Mens' literature; 2. Death and dying; 3. Ecopsychology;
4. Literary commentary

LCCN: 2003105871

CIP

Edited and designed by Sarah Felchlin
Front and back cover computerized images by Emerald North.

Graphics excerpted from:
Heck, J.G., *The Complete Encyclopedia of Illustration* (London: Merehurst Press, 1988)
Gayley, Charles Mills, *Classic Myths in English Literature and in Art* (Boston: Ginn and Company, 1911)

First Edition
Manufactured in USA

For Meredith, Kevin, Dorothy, Matthew, Scott, David, Shelley, Mike, Michael, Morgan, Greg, Keenan, Patricia, Olivia, Christian, Selene, Howard, Michelle, Johnny, Katie, Eric, Jeff, Jennifer, Drew, Marley, Catie, Gregory, Shay, Meegan, Arwen, Marilyn, John, Matthew, Emily, Win, John, Jesse, Susannah, Gigi, Winslow, Warren, Winifred, Tom, Garland, Haiko, and Markus.

And for the gifted woman who midwifed this book from the body of the electronic Cyclops—

Sarah Felchlin

ITHAKA

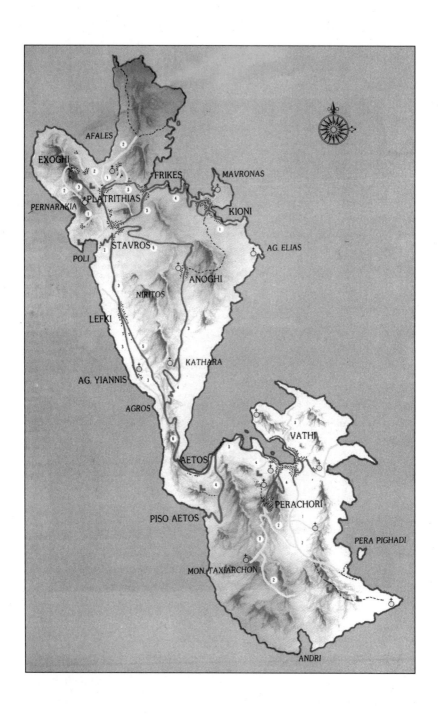

FOREWORD

THERE ARE OLD THINGS ON THE ISLAND OF ITHAKA. Earthquakes have buried most of them, in the land or under the sea. But the glint of the ancient may be seen here and there, in a terraced hillside, in a flake of pottery washed up by a storm. Since the excavations of Troy, Mycenae, and Pylos, groups have come to Ithaka, looking for the castle of Odysseus, lured by reverence or avarice, to the king's ransom the hero is said to have brought home from Corfu, island of the alluring Nauusika of the white arms. But the castle has never been unearthed, and Ithaka has never been counted among the islands rich in archeological lore. In the 1950s and 1960s, a German archeologist argued with considerable force that the neighboring isle of Lefkas was the true Ithaka of Homeric history. He never found the castle of Odysseus there, though he died trying.

An archeologist from England lived on Ithaka for ten years, they say. She stayed long enough to furnish a couple of small museums with tantalizing samples of the island's past, as far back as 2500 B.C. The local people claim that she stole more than she left, and that among her finds were numerous vases of great value, gold coins and other objects of marvelous and ancient craftsmanship that are strikingly unlike comparable artifacts found on Kephallinia, the larger island to the south. If what they say is true, then the woman should be drummed from her profession for making discoveries she couldn't tell the world for fear her thievery would be revealed.

While we were living there, the locals kept fantasizing that Capt. Jacques Costeau would soon anchor "Calypso" in the harbor at Stavros to investigate reports that thirty meters below, in the crystal waters of the bay, a sunken *polis* (city) existed, virtually untouched by Italian or French scavengers. The rumor of Costeau's presence was good for the island. What he found he gave to the Greek people. But Costeau never did any serious excavations in Stavros. For one reason or another, myths-archeology tends to look elsewhere. Ithaka is, after all, a rather unpromising-looking little island.

The latest excavations, begun in 1984 by Professor Sarantis Symeonoglou of Washington University in St. Louis, are centered in the high saddle between Mt. Neriton and Mt. Aetos, and cover more than 100 acres. Thousands of artifacts have been unearthed there, including the remains of the sanctuary of Apollo (XXIV, 475), the fountain known as "Clearwater" (XVII, 261-9), the *agora* (marketplace), and the tantalizing remains of what apparently was a theater. The professor is confident that eventually he will discover the ruins of Odysseus' great hall, which, according to the Homer's song, was located at a distance from the town now known as Stavros.

The island of Odysseus will yield her secrets conservatively. But the palace will eventually be found. It's obvious to anyone standing above Stavros looking out to the northwest. The mountains on either side form a woman's thighs open to the western sky. In the middle is an upraised mound, the *mons veneris* as seen from the belly, pointing out across the channel toward Kephallinia. Why would anyone look anywhere else for the castle of Odysseus, the angry man in every man?

The people of Ithaka speak fondly of Odysseus. They are proud to own him as an ancestor, though most of them have no real idea who the mythical/historical man was. They are mildly concerned about the archeological thefts from their island. They are far more concerned with the day-to-day problems of survival. One can hardly blame them. The earth is rich but grudging. "No one would use this ground for training horses; it is too broken, has no breadth of meadow," but "there is nothing meager about the soil." Cut off from the fertile Peloponnisos by 40 miles of open, sometimes impassable *thallasa* (ocean), the island is subject to earthquakes, fierce gales, and weeks of rain. In 1953, a temblor (6.8), levelled 80 percent of the houses, and tremors are an everyday occurrence.

Recently, despite an outflux of the young to seek their fortunes elsewhere, good progress has been made toward the realization of island pride in its heritage. Periodically, summer groups of scholars come to meet together on the island. Occasionally, there are theatrical and cinematic festivals, also during the summer, when the population swells to twice its normal size. Many South African and Australian Greeks return to repossess their homes when the weather turns warm and the sea becomes friendly.

The village we lived in was quite small. The permanent population was 300. It seemed one of the loveliest villages in all the Greek islands, a typically Ithakan village, though each village on the island had a different personality. Indeed, Kionion was so fascinating a world that I could almost forget Odysseus. We marvelled daily at the drama of participatory survival unfolding around us—the ways in which these people interrelated and assumed the roles most likely to personally and collectively insure the maintenance of life. Community. Home. Thus Kionion perpetuated herself for thousands of years, surviving wars, pirates, natural disasters, and the national pastime of politics—breeding a passionate intelligence yoked improbably to a stubborn, independent pride.

My son, Keenan, age 12, crossed the sea in a Boeing 707 to be with his father and step mother in Kioni. I'll never forget the day he swam out into the little bay with a bread knife and, repeatedly diving, brought back an octopus for dinner. He was a tall lad, full of ginger, with the need to prove himself as a man. He did so to the amazement of the Greek men who watched from the tables at the local taverna. They marvelled at this demonstration of the prowess of the pubescent American male. It was a kind of passage rite, similar to the spear hunt of young Odysseus, when he was gored by a rampaging boar. But there was a difference. It wasn't a copper-tipped spear, but a bread knife that did the trick. And Keenan, now a married, ardent bio-ecologist of endangered species, with a blond, Anglo-Saxon daughter, swears up and down he has nothing to be proud of.

There is no doubt that King Odysseus walked along this bread knife bay. He must have foraged his goats above Kioni, threshed his wheat, picked his olives and apples, and reaped his wine. Divers still find amphorae in the emerald waters of the tiny cove. Fishermen still use the old methods of net and lamp light to catch *calamari*, "tuna," and needlefish. Women still pick the olives and stomp the grapes. There may be television sets and an occasional telephone, but the ancients persist in their ways of life, a true ancestral heritage. The old fisherman with a glint in his eye says he knows all about Odysseus—but he thinks the best story is about Odysseus's other son by Circe, the one who was murdered by Telemachus over there on the little island of Asteris. Odysseus, he says, lived in Stavros and at the harbor there was a village and a wharf, and in the old days the hillsides were thick with pine, hemlock, olive, and oak, and in the small steep canyons grain was sown. And springs, like the one at Ag.Iohannes, cascaded from crevices above Stavros, and Kionion too, and down-island at Arethusa. But the earthquakes stopped them up.

A shrewd-faced little man unlocked the museum in Stavros for us one day. The place was a mess. It looked as though a caged dog had tried to get out. The last entry in the register was a month ago (a couple from Australia). On the floor, in a thousand pieces, lay the remains of three precious jugs fashioned before Christ was born. The man surveyed the carnage with mild shock and anger. "Seismos," he muttered. "Poor little island home," I thought, "beset by earthquakes and greed."

The display was modest, except for some pieces of jewelry over 3,000 years old. One object caught our eye—a Mycenean plate of the most exquisite manufacture, intricately glazed and painted with fabulous creatures, suggesting Egypt, Crete, and golden sunburned lands. Cracked and incomplete, the object alone was a priceless reason for doing exhaustive archeological work at Stavros. The man pulled us about, explaining this and that. He was very kind to us.

Afterward, he took us to the top of a knoll from where we could see the Ithakan Channel, the Lefkadian Channel, and the Ionian Sea. On the way down, we stopped at the ruins of an old church, and looked around while, in a corner, he lit oil wicks in their wind-proof chambers. A fat orange cat slunk through the broken walls. Half-wild, he looked us over from a distance and then followed us back to the car. It was beginning to rain. The scent of anise and apple lay fresh on the southeast wind. The olive trees were bending, exposing their silvery underflesh. Autumn rains were slanting down, awakening meadows with dandelion, cyclamen, and daisy. It was easy to imagine that Homer, or Odysseus, or some similar liar-king-adventurer-father-husband-friend of the goddess, called this place home.

Then where are his bones? Where was the great man buried? Who cares—except for all the civilized world, the very world that this little island, tilted up from the sea, gave birth to. I care. We all care, all of us angry men who dream of coming home. And so the foundation of the western world has been established and nurtured by this ageless story — and the story goes on and on—of our fathers and grandfathers who have lived and come home. Surely, somebody will care where our bones lie buried. Surely, somebody will care where we finally came to rest.

Somewhere lie the bones of Odysseus. On Kephallinia? No. On Lefkadia? No. On Scorpios? No. On Krete? No. At Troy? Absolutely not. Where then?

On Ithaka.

On the road winding north along Phorkys Bay—where our hero, after twenty years of hardship and wandering, first set foot on his native soil—a nightmarish Fiat came tumbling around a blind corner and nailed our Volkswagen bus against a wall of death.

But it was not our time. Fate would not allow my woman, pregnant with our daughter, to die. We survived the accident and the curious and sympathetic Greeks who swarmed about the scene. We survived to live another day, and then to board a 707 bound for the New World.

Meanwhile, the waves curled in on the shore like days torn from an endless calendar, and the grey-eyed sea owls screamed and dived, and olive trees grafted from the olive trees of Odysseus' great grandchildren hissed in the ocean wind.

June, 1976

Twenty-five years later my woman and I visited Ithaka again, this time with our children and grandchildren, to celebrate Meredith's 50th birthday.

Things had changed. Yachts crowded the little harbor of Kioni, and throngs of tourists caroused in not one but four tavernas. The village had changed forever. Now it was rich with the money of tourists, and the stone shell of a house in which we had lived so many years ago had been converted into a fine dwelling place complete with electricity, heat, kitchen, bathroom (flush toilet!), and running water. The man who lived there, formerly with the Greek National Theater, welcomed us in and recounted the history of the house, which included a strange story about an American couple who had lived there long ago, and as the legend went, conceived a child in the cold, empty upper bedroom.

In the oldest taverna, festooned with photographs of visitors to the island, was a faded photo of Meredith and me at a local baptism. The *mitera* came to our table, picture in hand, and stood by smiling as we marvelled at the passing of years. Then the same little boy who had been baptized, now a strapping man of 25, approached us with a shy greeting. His name could have been Telemachus, but it was Nikos, and his father had died years before of a heart attack. Now he helped his mother run the taverna and occasionally went fishing. Proudly, he pointed to his boat riding the gentle waves of the little harbor. I asked him how good was the fishing. He said, "Very poor. There are no more fish left."

That same night our children and grandchildren treated us to a boat ride, with a bottle of wine and an old fisherman friend, who remembered us from way back. He rowed the boat from the harbor to the edge of the open *thallasa* while we reminisced and looked back at the lights of the little town dancing on the water. The moon above us was almost the same full moon we had seen 25 years before, the night we named the child in Meredith's womb, *Selene*.

June, 2001

Most scholars consider Homer to be a poet who lived in 7th century B.C. No doubt he was the "channel" for many traditional legendary songs about this archetypal hero, extending back into Greek history for many centuries. Homer was the one who gathered all this ancestral memory together into a coherent tale and gave the whole an exquisite lyrical voice. Tradition persists that he was blind. This disability gave him the ability to inwardly see in vivid detail by repeating certain symbols and archetypes that continually inform the narrative line.

It was then I understood—thanks to you,
home-abolisher—that Ithaka does not exist.
The only thing that exists is the sea, and a barque
as tiny as a man's body, with Mind as captain.

– Nikos Kazantzakis

TABLE OF CONTENTS

"Sing in me muse, and through me tell the story." Homer, *The Odyssey*, (I, 1)

The year I left college, my brother Greg gave me a book that changed my life. It was a translation of *The Odyssey* by Robert Fitzgerald, my poetry teacher at the University of Washington. From the moment I opened this great legacy of our sacred ancestors, I was spellbound. Never after able to put it down, the story relentlessly sought me out and found me in the sacred chambers of memory—and thrust a tear-sword into my soul. I must have read it fifty times, and every time I wept and put it down—only to take it up again as time and opportunity permitted. Twenty-five hundred years of human history wouldn't let me go. Those years vanished the moment I re-read the first sentence. The story wasn't about the "good old days" when men heroically contended with the gods. It was about today—about you and me—about how it feels to be a man.

Forty years later, still longing for home, I take up the pen to write about *The Odyssey*. Forty years of wandering. Forty years of grief. Forty years behind the tiller on the open sea, drifting with the fickle winds and currents of life, contending, grieving, losing, finding. Forty years in the boudoir of the witch. Forty years of lying, stealing, plundering, shape-shifting, forty years of playing the fool. Forty years of nymphs and underworlds and passages and tests and comrades and ghosts. Forty years of trying to get back to my sons and daughters. Forty years of longing for my woman, for the secrets of our bed, and the ultimate fulfillment of home.

Now, all those years of wandering have coalesced into this Phaeacian ship with black sails, in which I lie, looking up at the night sky, heart-heavy with the treasures of a lifetime of grief—no more than a few hours from the rocky slopes of Ithaka. Calmly, the crew goes about their collective task, setting and trimming the sails, steering by the beacon of the Great Wain. They too know the taste of disappointment and grief, and the ecstasy of waking up at dawn, their lovers by their side. Pale nymphs crowd around, seeing in me the man of their dreams. But I know better. No matter which goddess or god I slept with, I always knew what I really wanted. As sleep tugs at my eyes, I whisper a prayer to the woman who has made all the difference: "If I have been untrue . . . it was never to you."

Men sometimes speak well of me in the councils. I am content with that, and I know none of this approval will mean a blessed thing when, for the last time, I stand tall in the hall of the suitors and nock the arrow of destiny to the bowstring of life. The battles, the enchantments, the doldrums, the comrades brave and free, the truths and lies, the lonely years, will come to me in the *here and now*, and amount to nothing, if I cannot string the bow.

As the black ship, like "a four horse team, whipped into a run on a straightaway, shows her heels to the swell," I fall asleep. Despite all those days of breasting wave-roads, my mind is finally at rest. Soon I will land on my rocky island home. A great struggle awaits me there. Before the gates of death I will fight the good fight. When and if the battle is won, I will inherit the secret bed. And then I will carry my oar far away from the ocean of strife.

One last time I will take a stand against those karmic monsters who threaten my homecoming, knowing full well they are my just desserts. Long ago I decided to go off to the war. I could have said no. I could have convinced those who called me that I truly was insane. No doubt I was crazy, or believed myself to be, as I plowed the beach and sowed salt seeds. But I couldn't resist the call. I had to learn that such decisions have consequences, not the least of which were grievous troubles, murderous dangers, and separation from those I loved the most.

How many times, drifting in the "solid deep-sea swell, awaiting death," did I mindlessly boast about my prowess to the god of earthquakes? This macho vain glory gave me nothing but heartache. Again and again the Earthshaker moved against me: "Go on, go on, wander the high seas this way, take your blows, before you join that race the gods have nurtured. Nor will you grumble, even then, I think, for want of trouble."

But for now, "slumber, soft and deep, like the still sleep of death, closes my eyes as the ship heaves seaward." A goddess watches over me. Somehow I always knew it. She has been there all along, even in extremity, and has helped me through innumerable crises. Yet I keep complaining to her, "Where are you when I need you?"

Do I complain to her, or to myself?

"Rag of a man that I am, is this the end of me? I fear
the goddess told it all too well—predicting great adversity
at sea and far from home. Now all things bear
her out."

Blessed slumber falls like a starry night. There's nothing I can do
but surrender to the Muse of Dreams. In my soul I know she will convey
me to the lands where dreams forget.
Sing in me Muse.

"OF THESE ADVENTURES. . . TELL US IN OUR TIME. LIFT THE GREAT SONG AGAIN." (I, 17-18)

THE HISTORICAL EVENTS OF WHICH HOMER SANG occurred in the Mycenaean era, 400 years before he lived (circa 1250 B.C.), historically speaking, in "old Greece," (the earliest advanced Greek-speaking culture).

Shortly after the Trojan Wars, the Mycenaean empire and its cyclopean fortresses disappeared into the so-called "dark ages." For 400 years, petty chiefs, bandit gangs, scavengers, famines, and plagues harrowed the Mediterranean. Populations plummeted. Remaining Greeks fled to the Aegean and beyond. Culture appeared to vanish. And then a new era dawned, a renaissance dominated by Homer, the singer of the old tales of redemption and glory. Where did Homer get his stories? Did he make them up from nothing? Historical and archeological evidence says he sang of real events, of real men, humanized, mythologized, and filtered through hundreds of years of fireside telling.

Homer sang in archetypes. Of that we can be sure. But his archetypes differ somewhat from modern psychological archetypes. They are more rooted to the natural world, to the open sea, the forces and moods of nature, the basic, common feelings and sensations of men, seasoned by the darker, deeper mythical patterns of pre-Hellenic culture. The blood memory of untold centuries of males throbs in the great songs of Homer.

Of what is this blood song composed? The bed, the house, the island, the ancestors, the monsters, the fall from grace, the aging body, the old soldier, the root between the man's thighs, the blood debt, the angry man, the impatient wife, the husband, the son seeking his father, the lust-witch, the border of land and sea, the vision, the fool, the artist, the storm on the horizon, the anima, the animus, the stars, the "Nobody," the trickster, the shape-shifter, the goddess, and the friend of the goddess.

To whom is the song being sung? To men, and to the women of men, and to the sons of men who are men themselves, or men in the making—and even to those who aren't sure they have ever seen a man when they looked into the mirror. A song for men and women, an anthem, a story about how it is to live the life of a man. A song of fresh wind in the sails as we drift across great protagonistic seas, looking for our homes in caves of remorse and pig pens of witches, wrestling with drugs of forgetfulness and whirlpools of fear, lashed to the masts of our ships and trying oh so valiantly to ignore the sweet call of suicide!

The Odyssey is, no doubt, a kind of Tarot. At any moment you can throw down a random assortment of images upon an empty table and read the future of any man. There are the usual kings and queens and warriors and fools and witches and warlocks and falling towers and wine cups brimming and overturned. Death rides the wind and ghosts lust over spilled blood. Journeys begin and end, stars of hope spangle the sky and storms rumble with thunderbolts. Chariots clash in battle, spears and arrows fly, and lovers murder each other. Blind harpers sing, girls lose their virginity, and a boy becomes a man. Men go to hell and women wait and weave—and unweave. One woman stays faithful, and one man tries to make it home. Who would deny that such landmarks are familiar to men of heart and soul?

Pull a card from the deck and throw it down. Ah! The shipwrecked sailor!

"Such desire is in him merely to see the hearthsmoke leaping upward from his own island, that he longs to die." (I, 78-80)

I'll never forget the night we were driving home from the Southern Mojave and a snow storm hit us, the kind that happens every fifty years. Mile after mile we slogged through the clinging smother, the road turning softer, deeper, our windshield wipers clicking back and forth so faithfully until, no more than 30 miles from our home at Three Creeks, a gust of wind tore the wiper on the driver's side clean off the car.

It had been a difficult time away from home. The stress of being with other people had affected my ability to breathe. Ancestral genes were eating away at my lungs. The doctors were saying things like "irreversible but not immediately deadly." Things were getting worse but I could still get around without oxygen bottles during daylight hours. My image of myself at the moment the wipers blew away was pretty much governed by such bodily weaknesses as my 60+ years had instilled in me.

Suddenly, I felt all alone. It was I who was dying, not the woman at my side. She was in perfect health, a fact on which my own survival now depended. Panic struggled up from my lungs into my throat and death felt very near. I wanted more than anything else to reach home, somewhere out there in the snowy darkness, interminable miles ahead. All we had to do was get there.

The ghost of Odysseus appeared in the car then. All those years he had been trying to come home. He had tried so hard he "longed to die." But I didn't want to die. I wanted to get home so that I could live. What was this "longing to die?" What had it to do with longing to live? Were the two longings, in fact, similar?

I should have pulled over. Driving had become unsafe. Our lives were in jeopardy. But I didn't pull over to wait for someone to rescue us. Absurdly, I pulled out my bandanna, opened the side window, and began to wipe the snow from the windshield, back and forth, a human robot-wiper. After a minute or so, my hand began to freeze.

Mile after mile crept by. I cussed and panted while my woman, in alarm and sympathy, watched me struggle to keep a tiny patch on the windshield clear. She too wanted to get home, and was trying to steer me from her side, where the wiper was still working. But the snow kept falling and it was getting scary and my arm was so tired and the bandanna was heavy-wet and freezing and my muscles were tense and shaking.

I wanted so badly to get home that I was ready to die.

At a certain point we began to look for the familiar turn-off sign. It seemed like forever, and when we finally left the highway, and headed down that last leg for home, I was both living and dead. I had died to live so that I could be born again at home. When we pulled in the driveway, I knew that dying to live and living to die were one and the same. And that the bridge between the worlds was called home.

Homer knew it so well. All the poets knew it too. Drunken old Dylan Thomas knew it when he said, "The force that through the green fuse drives the flower . . . is my destroyer." That force is none other than our "longing to see the hearthsmoke leaping upward from our own island."

"ODYSSEUS WAS NOT THE ONLY ONE AT TROY NEVER TO KNOW THE DAY OF HIS HOMECOMING. OTHERS, HOW MANY OTHERS, LOST THEIR LIVES!" (I, 405-407)

I WAS A HIGH JUMPER IN COLLEGE. Not an especially good one, but I loved the sensation of defying gravity, if only for a short while. But I could never clear six feet, no matter how I tried. I fell face-first into the sawdust with the dislodged crossbar and lay there, wondering if I would ever make it home.

Six feet was, in fact, my own height. I was measuring myself, my myth, by how high I could jump. And I was never quite able to clear my own height.

Nevertheless, I did not die in the lists at Troy. Why? Didn't I deserve to be reaped by the Fates? Not strong or agile enough to clear the bar? A part of me is deeply ashamed. Many others who could clear the bar were taken, long before they had any chance to reach the island of their dreams. Yet I found a way to clear my own height without jumping, and now I am within a few miles of home.

How many have fallen short of their homecoming! Or is death itself the homecoming? What is more important? Clearing the bar or biting the sawdust? Homer seems to imply that clearing the bar is the only way to reach home. Those who fall short—and even those who possess the psycho-physical ability to soar far beyond their own height—are reaped by the sawdust of death while Odysseus miraculously lives. Why? Does the old blind man Homer imagine that there are certain men who can cheat, defy, challenge, overcome, the inevitability of death? If so, he is as big a fool as I am.

In Hebrew, *homer* means "measure of capacity." Capacity for what? Does it matter if we clear the bar? Does it matter if we advance against the bombs and bullets of the enemy, peeing in our pants, fail to clear the bar, yet manage to survive somehow? Does it matter if, with the purest of convictions, we advance against the hail of death and die of shrapnel to the heart? The conflict always comes to the same conclusion. Sawdust.

Some came home from Troy. Some did not. Among those who managed to reach home were many not especially favored by the gods. Home was not what it had been. Penelope was not necessarily the faithful wife. And many a son who had set out to find his father, had his throat slit by bandits and drug addiction. This Troy business is risky for father, mother, and children. First you have to get there. Then you have to ride your chariot into battle against overwhelming odds. Then you have to find your way home.

Why should any of us imagine we are among the favored ones?

"EVERY DAY SHE WOVE ON THE GREAT LOOM — BUT EVERY NIGHT BY TORCHLIGHT SHE UNWOVE IT."
(II, 112-13)

IN HOMER'S DAY, THE WOMEN OF GREECE WERE WEAVERS. They stayed at home and kept the home hall together and made it beautiful for themselves, their husbands and children. Only in Sparta were they allowed to assume male roles. Nevertheless, the women of Greece kept the uneasy "nation" of city states whole. The Golden Age would not have lasted so long if it had not been for the labors of women who safeguarded the castles and lands while their husbands went off to senseless wars. The people would never have made it through the dark ages if the mothers and daughters had not prevailed.

Penelope's tapestry on the great loom is one of Athena's greatest archetypes, for it was the goddess who invented the loom. That same goddess finally had her way with the patriarchal god, Poseidon, who resisted her desire to rule Athens. When he caused a salt-water spring to flow on the Acropolis, she made an olive tree grow. Her way was to bring life, not death, to the people. It was she who taught the women how to weave baskets and mats and blankets and clothing and curtains and tapestries and all those household necessities that contain, cover, and sustain.

Who is Penelope? Is she nothing more than a flat stereotype of the faithful wife? Only in so far as marital love can be constant throughout a life. Only in so far as the inescapable truth that some humans mate for life. No doubt she was not the "perfect, faithful wife." In a symbolic way, she is Mother Earth herself, weaving the intricate tapestry of life and then unravelling it in death.

Mythologically, Penelope was the daughter of a Spartan king violently opposed to her marriage to a young upstart from the tiny kingdom of Ithaka. The love-smitten Odysseus finally confronted her: Your father or me? Silently veiling her girlhood face, she chose Odysseus. This veil of mystery over the face of the daughter who the father has loved so well cannot be torn away by sarcasm. Indeed it is true that some women commit themselves to their man forever. In Classical Greece, that was so. In modern times, it is also so. Some women wait. And even though great and terrible

wars have been fought by men over the honor of an unfaithful woman, there has been many a woman who waited for her man to come home.

What is this thing that Penelope weaves on the great loom? Clothes for a dead man, for her father-in-law, Laertes. But the old man wasn't dead yet. In fact, he would live to see the return of his son and would even slay a man in the final battle for his estate. So Penelope would never finish the shroud while the suitors were still in the house. They tried to make her finish. They gave her an ultimatum; they said: "We have found you out. You have been tricking us. Finish the shroud or decide who will be your next husband." But she refused them. Every night she pulled the threads from the work of the day.

Can it be that the clothing our mothers began to weave for us when we were living in her body is this very shroud? That this shroud is being spun for our fathers by our grandmothers? That this shroud will not be finished until we have come home finally and stand together as father and son to defend the family legacy?

The shroud is home—the cocoon for all living beings in the universe. Our cocoon. Our father's cocoon. Our grandfather's cocoon. The cocoon earth has woven for us. The cocoon she unwove every night so that she could start from the beginning again to weave for us our death clothing. And then, all at once, finally and abruptly, the shroud is completed —and we go, wrapt in a shroud of glory.

The body is a very strange thing. Day by day it renews itself. But as the years pass, ever so slowly, the Weaver, with cunning fingers that refuse to dissolve from the material, gradually creates an image, a picture, a story. And when the time is nigh, the picture, under nimble threads, becomes complete. But it won't happen until Odysseus, the rover, the angry one, comes home.

Should we not pray then, to the goddess in our Penelopes, and beg her to love the picture she is weaving into our shrouds? Every step we will take is a stitch made and unmade—and so we will complete our picture on the great loom. There she will wrap us up in her finished clothing and take us to some place far inland, where nobody ever heard of the sea.

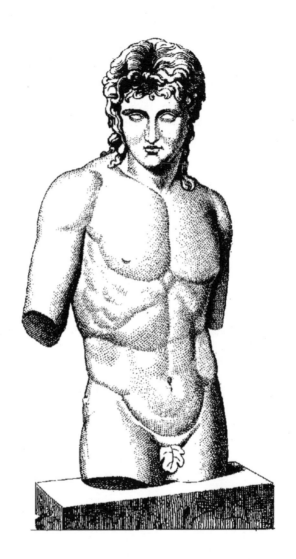

"THE SON IS RARE WHO MEASURES WITH HIS FATHER. . . BUT YOU WILL HAVE THE SAP AND WIT AND PRUDENCE."
(II, 292-4)

HOW IS THE SON TO KNOW THAT HE MEASURES UP to his father? Even a goddess can remind him of the fine stuff of which he is made and he will not believe her. He must find out for himself. He must watch himself behave when the chips are down, at the man-making moments of truth, in order to consider himself the equal of his father. Until then, everything is vanity and uncertainty. No doubt he can boast of his power and courage to the skies—but he will never know for sure.

According to Athena, signs of the attainment of manhood are "sap" and "wit" and "prudence." Sap is the blood of vegetation, the essence of well-being. Wit is intelligence, wisdom, cleverness, and the ability to shift shape. And prudence is discretion, sound judgment, sensibility—look before you leap. Such attributes do not come easily to the brash young sons of their fathers, but are only gained through experience. How is the young man to know if the stuff in his veins is invigorating sap or aimless energy? Only by putting the ancient memories in his veins to use. How is the young man to know if he has wit when the world around him seems witless? Only by considering the relationship of witlessness to wisdom. And how is he to know if he is prudent when all the world seems to be luring him into indiscretion? Only by going ahead and learning control.

An adolescent boy does not know how to change his shape to suit the occasion. He can put on all kinds of costumes and try out all kinds of personae, and probably will, for adolescence is the time to be outlandish, to stick out like an index finger held high, to be "seen" and "talked about" by peers. He is still profoundly under the sway of convention. He stubbornly holds on to customs of his "friends," his hair style, his hat, his tattoo, his lingo, his "personality." As time goes on, he may learn that there are far more productive, and creative, ways to hide his ego, to subtly alter his personality, even to become invisible.

By "wit," the goddess is referring to the prudent use of sap. It does absolutely no good to explode in adolescent anger, to pout, or deny, or be macho, or resist in one way or another. Or would it be far more appropriate to catch the sap of fiery anger in a cup of reasonable words, and thus avoid unnecessary unpleasantness? Do I shift my sap-shape and become one of the nicest guys the policeman ever stopped? I might even get away with a warning.

When youthful elan is challenged by the numberless realities of life and pressed into the service of prudence, we become capable of merging with—and therefore changing—our reality and environment. If we hold ourselves apart from the "game," and from our own humanity, our chances for survival lessen considerably. We could be in danger of never becoming men, or of becoming boy's psyches in the bodies of men.

Those who hate without thought are too eager to become bombs. Bombs kill innocent people. Those who can shift from hatred to wit don't have to become bombs. The true male warrior is a man of many faces, and each face is a way of finally making it to his rocky little island home, where his faithful lover waits for him with their children standing by her side.

Of course, the goddess was fudging a little about how prudent and wise father Odysseus had actually been. After his perfect ruse of escaping from the blinded Cyclops by hugging the belly of sheep, the old guy boasted to high heaven that "It was I, Odysseus, who took your eye." The fool came out from under the disguise of "Nobody" and blew his pat little universe all to hell. He let the sap flow without mitigating prudence. He doomed every one of his shipmates to death.

Can we fault the man for that? I have never known a man, even the most mature man, who didn't at one time or another slip up, seriously. I mean, really seriously. Nevertheless, the goddess loved him. She told his son that he looked like his father!

How fortunate we are to be loved by a goddess! Her love allows us to take a long time to inherit our manhood—long after our shallow culture pronounces us men.

"NEVER, ANYWHERE, HAVE I SEEN SO GREAT A LIKENESS IN MAN OR WOMAN. . . THIS BOY MUST BE THE SON OF ODYSSEUS." (IV, 152-4)

WHEN I WAS THE REBELLIOUS ADOLESCENT SON just entering the passage to manhood, I swore I would never be like my father. Forty-five years later, I can see what happened to that naive resolve. I was never able to rid myself of his body. I became an ectomorph, like him, and grew the same chin, jaw, hair, eyes, adam's apple, shoulders, back, teeth, feet, legs, ankles, and ass. I smile like him and move around a room like him and even talk with the same tone of voice. As I grew older, I realized I had inherited his bodily weakness, especially his lungs. Other characteristics as well: spare tire, weak ankles, weird toes, high arches, dark hair, nearsighted eyes, ears prone to deafness, and a restive digestive tract. There is nothing like aging to bring out all the physical similarities.

 Psychologically, the likenesses between the man I became and the father by whom I was raised were far more difficult to trace. On the one hand, we shared certain emotional characteristics—ways of holding in or expressing anger; pride in our place, work, and families; egotistical stubbornness; sense of humor; etc. These kinds of shared personality traits were many and diverse. For instance, my wife repeatedly identifies a certain way I have of blowing small matters into big ones and loudly "quitting the game" in order to get ready to play it, as characteristic of my father.

On the other hand, much of my psychological makeup seems quite different from my father's. Apparently, my experience of life pushed different buttons than his. I had to piece together a host of different "complexes" in order to psychically survive the passages. These complexes, or puzzle pieces—call them "archetypes"—have become very important windows on my soul. How important? *All Important.*

It would seem this is true of any father's son. We grow our own soul. It doesn't have anything to do with "looking like our fathers." Fathers and son share alike in this privilege. And in the end it matters not what our fathers do to us, or don't do to us. We develop a soul independently from them, yet with certain identifiable threads of similarity that we must bear with a certain amount of ironic pride. Okay, Dad, if I can't entirely do away with you in me, at least I can let it be, perhaps even appreciate it.

I was talking with a man today who does not know his father. Forty-five years ago he was born a "bastard" and an orphan. And all this time he has been unconsciously looking for his father. This might be hard for him to accept. Underneath the incredible ways in which he has "made" himself, there is an absolutely righteous anger at his father for not showing up after all that searching. I value this man. He has become a true individual, apart from any parent, family, or lineage. He is a survivor. His soul teaches my soul.

I love to experience Tom's "character." He's quite a mystery. Somewhere in him is the ghost of his father. I want to tell him something that is ancient and very true, that he is a noble man, from a noble line, among whom are kings and princes and magicians and clowns and warriors and holy men. I want to tell him that I see his father in him.

But I have to leave that task to the goddess. Or as Homer has it, I must leave this task to Helen, coming from her sacred chamber "straight as a shaft of gold." I must allow her to deliver the punch-line:

"Never, anywhere, have I seen so great a likeness in man or woman."

"How easily one can tell the man whose father had true felicity, marrying and begetting."
(IV, 223-4)

My father was a good man, but I hardly knew him. I lost him when he was converted to evangelical Christianity. I was 13 at the time, and had already begun to sin in ways that were abhorrent to his God. Rejecting his faith, I sallied forth into the trials of manhood without his favor. Rudderless, I drifted on the ocean of life. Again and again I landed on strange islands where nobody had news of my father. Again and again I stuck my innocent nose into Cyclops' cave. Again and again I woke up in Circe's pigpen. Again and again I was cast adrift at sea. How fortunate I was that the goddess Athena took pity on me!

She took the form of mentors who, at crisis moments, helped me to see what I had to do. Basically, my course was simple. I had to find my way back to my father. But the way was fraught with monsters, the same monsters by whom I had already been wounded: overweening pride, memories of his brutality, memories of loss of favor, anger at his "authority," and for his worship of the Protestant Zeus (as opposed to Athena)—anger so strong that I might have wished him dead.

I know I am not alone in this absolutely necessary search for the father. One of my best friends, a former All-American linebacker, a lieutenant-colonel in the Marine Corps, a veteran of two hitches in Vietnam, is on the same journey. Our fathers are dying. They are finally coming home. And all that searching for news of them has brought us to the most important opportunity of our lives—to somehow meet them, soul to soul, after long last, and to stand with them to defend our ancestral inheritance.

Now I see the goodness of my father, the complicated beauty and courage of his lifelong quest for truth. Set adrift on the Great Depression and shipwrecked off the coasts of two World Wars, he encountered the Sirens and bedded down with Circe. Bereft and battered, he endured the loneliness of innumerable nights at sea, having deliberately pulled up anchor in the tempestuous regions of faith in his God. He too has known fear and anger and misery and hope, and has gone to the ends of the earth to find Penelope, his sons and granddaughters, and the inheritance he built with his own hands, waiting for him somewhere out there on that wide horizon. How can I deny him the fulfillment of this sacred searching?

I may not even recognize Dad when we meet. He may seem nothing more than an old man in rags. But give me time. Sooner or later I will remember the energy of him, the charisma, the character, the love-flame for my mother which he so faithfully tended all those years. I will recognize him because I will see how wrong I was to assume that my father had been lost at sea. And I will honor his God, the same God who placed all those obstacles, all those underworld caverns, all those trials and tribulations on the high seas, in my journey home.

We will embrace and smile into each other's eyes. Yes, it has been a long journey. Yes, we finally found the way home. Yes, we know so well that it was not our genes alone, but the genes of our mother and father, and of our mother's mother and our father's father, that brought us home in this condition. Thus it was ordained by the Great Creator. But this same Creator gave us the will to change ourselves, and to understand in our own way how to barter that inevitable journey.

Hello, father. How are you feeling? Yes, I left you long ago to find news of you. I regret nothing. I come from honorable stock. You raised me well enough, even when you were not there. How can I but love you with all my heart, now that we have both come home?

"THE MAN WAS BORN FOR TROUBLE."
(IV, 350)

THE WORD, "ODYSSEUS," IS FROM THE GREEK *odyssesthai*—"to hate," or "to be angry." Autolycus is said to have translated the name as "a victim of enmity." No doubt it has always been in the nature of a man to be angry, to feel victimized, to contest his fate with gods and men. He is just as quick to consider his own karma his enemy as he is to seize it as opportunity. The labyrinth he must negotiate in order to reach home all too often seems unreasonable, hopeless, and unjust. He blames the gods almost as much as he blames himself. But to publicly acknowledge his own complicity in what has come to pass is to admit his own weakness and stupidity. Caught in the Catch–22 of guilt, he erupts in helpless anger or invokes the gods of anger.

Odysseus well knew what he was getting into when he landed on the island of Polyphemos. From a distance he had watched that "brute so huge, he seemed no man at all" walking around like an earthquake. He'd even had a premonition that "Some towering brute would be upon us soon." It was his idea to take his best men and venture into the giant's lair and pilfer whatever wasn't fastened down. He paid the price: "No pretty sight, it turned out, for my friends." Two by two the monster cannibalized them, until only six of them remained.

If the gods don't bring it on, we bring it on ourselves. No matter how loudly we lament our fate, the truth remains. "The man was born for trouble." Leave your beautiful wife alone at home for twenty years, and you've got trouble. Fall asleep at the tiller, and you've got trouble. Kill the cattle of the sun god, and you've got trouble. Eat of the lotus, and you've got trouble. Blind the eye of Polyphemos, and you've got trouble. Mock the god of the ocean winds, and you've got trouble. Keep your arrows in your quiver, and you've got trouble. Pull them out, and you've got trouble. Keep your manroot hidden, and you've got trouble. Pull it out, and you've got trouble. Steer to the right, steer to the left, and you've got trouble. Do nothing, and you've got trouble. Keep devising ways of winning the game, and you've got trouble.

Who among us would be foolish enough to boast that we were free of trouble? We were all born for it. We make trouble wherever we go. Is it any wonder that we should be so angry, that we should want so badly to get home? But rage brings us no closer to our goal. Rage only twists us into ragged strangers begging at the back door. If we express our anger, if we lament our woes, we only attract more strangers with explosives taped to their bellies. Trouble goes where trouble is. And if we hold our anger in, letting it build within us, the caldera cracks open and we spew forth trouble like a pestilence. We murder, make war, raid cities, lay waste, enslave women, contend with one another, hurt the ones we love the most, and consume ourselves and each other with our refusal to admit guilt.

When the time comes, and it always does, for us to go into the cave where the blinded giant roars like thunder, there are but two options. One is to be eaten alive by adversity. The other is to trick trouble into letting us go for a while. I'm in favor of the second alternative, and am now convinced that the only way to get free is to admit, like Odysseus, that I am nothing—to say, "My name is Nobody: mother, father, and friends, everyone, calls me Nobody." So trouble, leave me alone for a while. I am, after all, not the least bit important.

Nobody is everybody. Not Bill, or Pete, or Odysseus, but any man who was born for affliction. Not the great so-and-so, but the generic asshole. The stupid, vain-glorious, egotistical asshole, like you or me. If we can cultivate this anonymous assholeness within ourselves, this acceptance of our karma, we may stand a chance in this life, and elude the fate of our brothers who were eaten alive.

"BUT YOU MUST HOLD ON, EVEN SO, AND CRUSH HIM UNTIL HE BREAKS THE SILENCE." (IV, 447-9)

AS THE FOAM HISSES PAST THE KEEL of the dark ship carrying me home, I wonder, sleepily, how men get to the truth. So much of what we face every day is nothing but deception and chicanery. So much depresses and deals death. So much, like sex, is here today and gone tomorrow, until not even the longing remains.

Do we wrest truth from illusion by brute force? After all, we are beings of muscular power and bone crushing violence. Surely, if we can smash, break, crush, obliterate, we can split the tangible down into smaller and smaller constituents until—until what? Until we see into the true life of things? We merely blast through illusions to new illusions and invent new names to describe them. The mystery remains. Even as I fall into sleep, something in me "knows" with a "regnant certainty" that the truth is much more than the physical world.

Okay. So maybe the truth is psychic. Maybe it lives in the multi-form images and feelings that compose the "psycho-memory" of the universe. Maybe the truth lives in the way entities remember and dream. Maybe it exists where ghosts move and control their material hosts. When I make love with my woman, she possesses me and I possess her. We both know that possession of each other's body is only part of what we seek. What we really want is to possess, for an aching moment, is each other's ghost, each other's soul—and to remember how perfect is this holding and letting go, this no and yes, this bondage and freedom. Surely, some of the truth lies here, in the roots of consciousness, in the psychic circles that ripple out from the act of love.

But try as we might to find the absolute verification of life's meaning, it eludes us again. The coyote becomes a lion becomes a serpent becomes a boar becomes water becomes gas becomes molecules become atoms become electrons . . . become . . . And so the shape shifting continues—in a thousand dimensions. The truth we stalk is more than human. And love is more than bodies rubbing together or souls being possessed.

The face of truth keeps changing, like a clown's, like our own face in the mirror. One minute we're smiling; the next minute we're crying. One minute we're getting a blow job and the next minute we're sitting with a friend who is dying. Is the truth nothing more than the fact that we are constantly shifting? Surely this is a fundamental law of the universe. Everything shifts its shape—entities, fields, theories, times, spaces, galaxies. Nothing, not even mathematical law, is free from principles of change.

If the Law is Change, then why are we still clinging like castaway sailors to pieces of wreckage we persist in calling the truth? And why do we keep telling ourselves that somewhere out there, or in here, there is a transcendental truth above or apart from time and space?

Despite all his fancy beliefs about Jesus the Son of God the Father and the promise of resurrection into Heaven when he died, my father was lonely. As he lay in a hospital bed at the end of a life strangely similar to that of Laertes, he was afraid. His faith had amounted to nothing. All he wanted was to be with my mother, who lay dying in another place. She was the "God" he wanted to go to when he died.

No matter how far and wide I am tossed by the winds of Change, I keep coming back to my own truth, to Now, when I must disappear from "this world." To me, the truth does not lie in the physical realm, or in the psychological synapse, or in the unchanging changing universe of mind. My truth exists in the moment of coming home, when I come face to face with . . . . what? Perhaps even then I will not know for sure.

Nevertheless, there is something in us, and outside us, that will not let us end this wandering until we have arrived at our destination—something that will not allow us to give up our strangle hold on God's angel of blessing, until we ourselves cry, "Enough!"

"Why has my child left me? Why did he go? . . . Must he, too, be forgotten?" (IV, 758-60)

Mama Penelope tends to overlook the obvious. Her son must sooner or later be given over to Mentor—i.e., Mother Earth/Athena /Great Anima. Because her husband has been gone for twenty years, she has had to care for him alone. All her frustrated love went into the boy. Why, she has had to be both mother and father to him!

It is absolutely imperative that Telemachus should embark on a voyage to find his father. He must leave mother's tender manipulations and experience the hard life of a sailor. He must find a ship and assemble a crew and sail for some fabled land for news of his father. He must meet his father's comrades at arms and see with his own eyes the fabled beauty of the woman whose dalliance with Paris caused men to go crazy with war.

He must be regaled with tales of his father, and in his imagination put himself in Dad's shoes. He must hear King Nestor's stories of the ill-fated Agamemnon. Polykaste, Nestor's lovely Lolita, must bathe the young man-in-the making, and rub his shy body with oil. He must experience the brilliance and opulence of the mansion of Menelaos at Pylos and hear first-hand how the red haired king won such treasure: "seven years at sea among the sun-burnt races." He must hear with his own ears the great king say, "No soldier took on so much, went through so much, as your father."

Helen must make a dramatic appearance from her "scented chamber, a moving grace like Artemis, straight as a shaft of gold," and turn her attention on the young man-to-be, and make him cry for the unattainable beauty of women. This same vision of grace must cry with amazement because the young man is, in fact, the true son of his father.

And then the inevitable initiation must be encountered. He must face the night passage of death, and find the wits to elude the suitors who wait in ambush. He must face this passage alone, with his brothers-in-arms, upon the open sea.

Such are the rites of passage to which every mother's son must be subjected.

Yes, mother, it is absolutely imperative that your son leaves home and travels far and wide for news of his father. His rite of passage into manhood must include other men, friends of his father, and beautiful women who inflame his senses and make him weep because of what is growing within him. He must see why his father chose these men and women to be his companions. He must recognize the legacy of his blood, of heroism, nobility, and generosity. No need for you to worry, dearest of mothers, about his safety. He is guarded by the same goddess who befriended you and your husband. In time she will show herself "in a clap of wings" and we will all see how truly well-favored is her son.

It is entirely possible that the boy will die and be forgotten. Many a young man (or woman) has disappeared into oblivion. Many a youngster has gone forth never to find father or mother. Many have gone forth to test themselves, only to fall prey to overreaching pride or insufficient self-honor. Many have succumbed to the highways of strange cities, or unfamiliar houses with uncaring companions unable to love them.

Penelope's fear is a deep one, and is felt in the guts of every man who aspires to accomplish something of lasting value. Will I make something of myself, as my mother hoped and my father resisted, or will I vanish without a trace into the tempest of time?

"Two nights, two days, in the solid deep-sea swell he drifted." (V, 405-6)

And then, at dawn of the third day, "breaking clear over a high and windless sea, and mounting a rolling wave," we catch a glimpse of land.

The Singer likens the feeling of sighting land to the emotions a man's children feel when, in his "extremity," he "recovers" from a long and "malignant illness." "His pangs are gone; the gods have delivered him."

It wasn't so long ago when I found myself castaway in the sea of a life threatening disease. One by one, the waves rolled over me. I could not set a course for myself. I was at the mercy of the tides, and I knew the drifting would bring me to death. Moments of terror became hours, days, and nights, bobbing and flailing in the terrifying swell. Finally, when it seemed I could not survive another wave, I glanced once more at the empty horizon and caught a glimpse of land.

How could I have known at that moment of relief that within the next 72 hours I would charm a princess, sway a king, win a battle of wits, bring tears to the eyes of a queen, tell a damn good story, and arrive at my very own home?

Ah, what do our children really know? Do they think we are finished just because we have succumbed to the drift? We may be getting old, but we are not done for. There's some kick left in the old dog. He can still sit up and wag his tail. He may have a distressing tendency to forget, but the goddess is on his side. She won't let him go before his time is up. And isn't it true that she is the one who laughs the loudest with joy when we return to the quest, and our children, seeing us rise up from the dead, realize anew, "what a dear, welcome thing life is?"

I have known this deathward drifting. After years of fasting alone in the desert, waiting for the end, I can say without equivocation, that letting go can lead to death. You want to live? Then get hold of yourself. Hold on to the tiller. Yes, I know that taking control is merely another form of drifting. But something very important within us makes us want to go down with a piece of the ship.

Don't give in to the storm. Hold on, even as the fury of the years tears you away. Be like the octopus: "When you drag one from his chamber, it comes up with suckers full of tiny stones." Leave "the skin of great hands" "on that rocky ledge as the wave submerges you."

Yes, your time will come. But not until you have come home. A shipwreck does not a death make.

Perhaps you heard of that fancy theory based on the idea that immersion in the death-element transforms us. When we make landfall, will the princess see us as "transformed?" Ah, she will do more than that. She will fall in love with us.

"NOW HE LOOKS LIKE ONE OF HEAVEN'S PEOPLE. I WISH MY HUSBAND COULD BE AS FINE AS HE." (VI, 258-9)

HOW LONG HAVE WE DENIGRATED, HATED, FLAGELLATED ourselves, because we were not the men our lover wanted us to be? How often did we forget who we were or could be? Because we saw girls, our women became girls. And because they saw boys, we became boys. The dance went on and on. It always took two to tango.

This game is very old, and has often been referred to as "the battle of the sexes." Humans were playing this game long before the Heroic Age of Greece. The Trojan War itself was fought by boys who could not see a faithless girl as anything more than a possession or a point of honor. A thousand ships launched in the name of honor! Menelaos is jealous: therefore we who trade and feast with him will risk our own lives to revenge our brother's honor, and steal back his (our) sacred image of girl. What kind of idiocy is this?

The return from Troy was equally disastrous. Agamemnon's girl-wife, Clytamnestra (from the Greek: *kleitoris*) was dallying with a treacherous boy-toy named Aigisthos, and together they devised a murder that lasted four hundred years:

> "Think of us, all fallen, our throats cut, winebowl
> brimming, tables laden on every side,
> while blood ran smoking over the whole floor."

One wonders just how many similar wars have since been waged, whether large or small, and how many lives have been snuffed out because the boy never became a man, nevertheless persisting that he was.

A true man is just trying to get home. He knows he will die someday, sooner or later. But all he really wants to do is reach the sunburnt crags of Ithaka and the woman who has waited for him all those years, the beautiful, faithful, devious, secretly erotic Penelope. These men are beloved by the goddess. These are the ones who will insure the survival of the human race.

Penelope can be a man—and Odysseus a woman. The wisdom of Homer's song goes far beyond sexual preference or gender. Penelope is the "loved one." Odysseus is the "lover." Both are full portraits of maturity; both throb with the dynamics of self-realization. In a world of gender-shifters, even the profane is sacred. Even the untractable wilderness of love can lead to the holy mountain. Only a man named Penelope can love. And only a woman named Odysseus can love. All the rest is the kind of infatuation that fuels the fires of war and genocide.

The song says that Odysseus emerged on the island of Scheria (Rhodes) after days of drifting at sea, with little more than a piece of mast to cling to. He had been to hell and back and was half-dead. The one who emerged from the breakers was no boy—but a man who had endured the wars of love. Each goddess he had left behind had given him a blessing, a teaching. His loving had not been in vain. He had learned his lessons. He knew what he wanted. The lover of his life was waiting for him.

It just so happened that a princess was there at the shore. Though not of "legal age" (according to modern law), she was beautiful and wise beyond her years. Behind his shield of olive branches she caught a glimpse of the naked, broken hero going home to his woman. She stood her ground with a bold heart and steady knees. "Turning, she called out to her maids-in-waiting: 'Stay with me! Does the sight of a man scare you?'" She could see that this was no ordinary boy-man.

And when the man emerged from his bath in the clothes the princess had given him, her girlhood dreams came true. The myth was real. Such men did exist. She wished out loud for such a husband. So lovely was Nausikaa, of "exquisite figure, as of heaven's shaping"—like those nymphs we old men see walking down the street, or standing in line before us in the store! Though our hearts heave a little with longing, knowing that possession of the body is forever unattainable, we can still appreciate the works of Mother Nature. Is it not true that something within urged us all those years to become that very man, though burdened by years of hard use, who prompted beautiful virgins to sigh and say, "Fare well, stranger; in your land remember me who met and saved you. It is worth your thought."

"HIS FATE HE SHALL PAY AT HOME, EVEN AS THE SPINNERS SPUN FOR HIM ON THE DAY HIS MOTHER BORE HIM." (VII, 211-12)

EVEN IN HOMER'S DAY THERE WAS NOTHING NOVEL about saying that what we do in life defines the way we die. Every religion says the same thing. With the sum total of everything we have been, we will cash in our chips. For each of us the dice roll comes up differently. You won't go the way I go. And I won't go the way you go. But we will all go.

Birth is not the beginning of our fate. The spinners have been weaving a life for us long before we were born. Our ancestors whisper in our blood. Our gifts are not ours, but theirs: feet and legs to balance on a pitching deck, arms and hands to hoist the sails, eyes and brains to navigate a featureless horizon, backs and shoulders to carry the burdens of another day, ears to hear the tears in cries of gulls, mouths to utter the deepest feeling and hope, hearts to sense the "mark twain" of love, and minds to follow the map of the stars—all these and so much more compose the bones upon which we flesh the mythic story of our lives.

Yet there are countless men who never become aware of these gifts, even in a lifetime. With lives so filled with strife and tragedy, they never wonder what magical stuff the spinners have spun into them. And then there are those who know, and even exercise these gifts, only to be disbelieved, ignored, or forgotten. How fortunate are the men who are not only able to use these gifts, but are honored among their brothers and sisters! Those who go unrecognized? Their spirit has simply been preserved for another day.

There is no way to avoid the truth of death—or of birth. If life confers on us certain "paths," death removes them. But death is not a thief. Death does not come like a thug in the night to rob us of our most sacred legacies. Death is an honorable and noble lord. Death knows that sooner or later we must enter his throne room and lay our tribute at his feet. Then it matters little if we have inherited a fleet or a piece of wreckage. Death graciously accepts it all. And on each of us death confers the privilege of going into that "good night" with the dignity of our forefathers.

It may be that from the beginning of life the way in which we finally come home is graven in our genes—a melody with a thousand variations. Perhaps its essence can be found in the song of the Sirens:

"Sweet coupled airs we sing.
No lonely seafarer
Holds clear of entering
Our green mirror."

How we allow ourselves to be drawn by the lure of one last despairing look into the mirror of nature! The poor, unsatisfied, unacknowledged, disappointed "I" will finally succumb to the truth of nature. If I must bow before the throne of Lord Death, give me one last chance to show who I really am!

Suicide is a justifiable alternative. But a more satisfying one is to finish the picture, at least until the paint runs out. Only then can we ask for help from the angels and pass through the throne room of death to join the spinners who spin and spin forever.

"A MOST UNLIKELY GOD AM I, BEING ALL OF EARTH AND MORTAL NATURE." (VII, 234-5)

WHY SHOULD KING ALCINOUS WONDER ALOUD if the shipwrecked stranger in his court was a god? Surely he knew better. Maybe he was the kind of king who considered any stranger to be a potential visitor from heaven. Odysseus was quick to deny any divine affiliation: "Rather, I am like those men who suffer the worst trials that you know, and miseries greater . . . Indeed, the gods could send no more." And then he fell to eating like any glutton, protesting that he was "mortal weary and sick at heart."

Nevertheless, there is an old truth in the ruler's words. Trials and tribulations ennoble us, even when we feel despicable in our own eyes. Those who are forced to endure the storms of life, who have travelled the shadow lands of misery, have caught a glimpse of sacredness unknown to men of ease. We wear the stains of star dust. Death has creased our mortal dress with the wrinkles of immortality.

Have you ever been "sick at heart?" Have you ever been overwhelmingly aware of your own mortality? Chances are you have. Some might find it difficult to boast of such experiences, preferring to keep their shields tight against their genitals. I have known such men, and have deeply respected them, despite their reluctance to speak of their own trials. Many are ashamed, imagining their difficulties to be silly, foolish, or inconsequential.

The fact is, Odysseus was a complainer. He was never able to hold back his self-pitying tongue when confronted by the gods. And to the extent that Homer is Odysseus, the poet is a complainer too. Certainly he had the right, being blind and old and buffeted by the tempests of man-life. Yet his blindness (and his self-pity?) ennobled him.

Life is no easier in the 21st century, even in the technocratic culture of a "privileged" country. We may be strangers to war and physical deprivation, but every day we wage the battles of mortality. Every day we sally forth into the ravages of routine, the antagonisms of the highway, the quicksands of the news, the conflicts of the sexes, the ill-will of fanatics, the shipwrecks of relationship, the fear of the unknown, the terror of terminal illness, the netherworlds of drugs and depression. There's nothing to be ashamed of. We have the right to complain. Jesus the son of God complained incessantly about the hypocrites. And when the chosen people turned away from God, He complained to Moses. And who was Moses? Just another angry, fallible Odysseus trying to get home to the promised land.

Many religions speak of gods who became human, and of humans who became gods. These opposite states of being seem to be the two sides of the same nature. Perhaps they are not so opposite after all. Sooner or later gods and humans come together to feast at the same banquet table. How are we to know who is who?

The Paiute Indians of our valley consider Coyote to be their god father. There is no doubt in their minds that their god can feel hunger and howl like any dog. There is great spiritual truth in Odysseus' declaration, that, after three days and two nights of fasting at sea, "There's no part of a man more like a dog than a brazen belly, crying to be remembered."

God feels hunger. God has been shipwrecked. God has drifted to the edge of death. God has gone without God. And God remembers. Because he remembers, we remember.

"You must have been the skipper of some tramp that crawled from one port to the next." (VIII, 171-2)

JOBS, VOCATIONS, PROFESSIONS—they are all worlds unto themselves, islands in the gulf stream, ports of call. We live in these lives for a while, and then we put out to sea, bound for other destinations. We grow older, enriched by shores upon which we have willingly visited, or landed by chance. Some of us have gone to war, enduring the horror of horrors. Others have fought in the streets, the ghettos, the neighborhoods, the universities, the work places—different kinds of wars, and sometimes on perilous psychological/spiritual soil. Veterans of multidimensional lives, we have learned wisdom, wit, and tact. Nevertheless, it matters little where we have been, when a brash, untried boy child, rippling with muscles, calls us an "old tramp."

No doubt it is in the nature of young men to be naive, to challenge the elders, to name themselves "Sea Reach" or "Shearwater" when they have never truly dared the mockery of a sea storm that blew them all the way to the gates of hell. We can smile inside because of what we know. Nevertheless, we are aghast at the lack of maturity among these adolescents. What fools they are! Are there no ways for them to prove themselves without making fun of those who have already put their lives to the test? Can't they understand there is "nothing like the sea for wearing out the toughest man alive?" We can only hope that their mythical names for themselves will propel them, like the winds of destiny, to mature wisdom.

> "Why do you young chaps challenge me?
> I have more on my mind than track and field—
> hard days, and many, have I seen, and suffered."

The years passed like storms and doldrums, seasoning us like old wine. Now we are more moved by the songs of the blind harper than by the boisterous cheers of the crowd. And when he sings of longing for home, we weep unashamedly—we, who have slept in the beds of kings and sipped from the lips of goddesses. Are we an old tramp? Yes, but an old tramp with memories so rich it would take a caravan a hundred miles long to carry them.

So what if we were cast upon an island dressed in nothing more than our birthday suit? A goddess loves us naked or clothed, rinses the salty crust from our limbs, and crisps our hair with the golden-red petals of the wild hyacinth. So what if we walk with a limp, or try to hide a swollen prostate, or creak with arthritis, or panic when we enter an enclosed space? She dresses us in the glory of her favor. We need no other badge of honor.

Even now, as the black ship carries us to one last, strange island, the goddess watches over us. I can only guess that again she will dress us in rags, that we will finally come home—infinitely more chastised than when we left—in the spitting image of an old hobo. Coyote will greet us at the door, and something about us, something reeking of strange ports of call and harrowing adventures, will make the old dog remember the young master who "wheedled" at the heels of his father in the family orchard, and hunted the wild boar on Mount Parnassos.

"INEPT AT COMBAT, AM I? NOT ENTIRELY." (VIII, 226)

HOW CAN IT BE THAT AFTER ALL THOSE DEFEATS my ego continues to stand up for itself like a knee-jerking penis? Sure, I've enjoyed a few victories, but never for long. This journey home has been hell, and I was always in the thick of it, enduring my share of hard knocks. Yes, I boast of Troy, but I have to admit Calypso, and the Cyclops, and Antiphates, and the Laistrogonians, and the Lotus Eaters, and the Sirens, and Scylla and Charybdis, and the cattle of Helios were not exactly victories. No doubt I fought as best I could, and I learned a hell of a lot about my capabilities. I've been knocked around like any other man.

How strange that I should still consider myself to be some kind of special person. Challenge me and I'm ready to make war in one way or another. I'd make a poor soldier? Well, not exactly. No doubt I've seen better days. Even if I can no longer lift my sword, I'll battle you with wits and shape-shifts. Don't count me out. Don't belittle me. A man still lurks behind this battered shield. I am not what I appear to be. I must insist. I am not what I appear to be.

I've had my share of contests. There were days when I quit the carnage as champion of the field. A man had been born in the lists of Troy, and the approval of the crowd lightened his footfalls. But just as often, I fell before the onslaught of events and beings far beyond my feeble control. If I know anything, it is the place the gods have given me in this life. Cyclops taught me that. Now you sit with me in council and bait me to compete in another contest? I reply: "You now, with your fine physique—a god's, indeed—you have an empty noodle. I find my heart inside my ribs aroused by your impertinence." And I rise again to the challenge of your "heart-wounding" words.

How strange that I still can feel avidness between my legs after all those nights I spent in the captivity of soft arms, after all those absurd ego-jousts. How many mornings did I weigh anchor when all seemed lost, my heart smarting with words that had been launched, like arrows, into the quick? The lessons of love were the hardest of all.

Then why does the magical discus still stand at ready whenever the love challenge comes? Well, *sometimes* ready. I have not always been willing to sally forth into the sweet and terrible fray. All too often I've stood before the chariot of love, trying to meet its onrush with my trusty sword, never even being sure it was I or her who had summoned me to the match. How long did it take for me to realize the miracle between my legs wasn't a sword at all, but a bodily extension of my heart? I should have known better. Don't tell me I didn't earn many a lesson! As the age of my heart expanded, so did the scar tissue around my cock.

Nevertheless, the question burns: why am I so eager to re-enter the lists of love—why, at this late date, when Ithaka is only a sleep away? Why do I continue to honor, even trust, the tired old Cassanova bumbling around inside my sagging skin?

You say "I never learned a sport, and have no skill in any of the contests of athletic love-men?" Not exactly.

"ALL MEN OWE HONOR TO THE POETS —
FOR THEY ARE DEAREST TO THE MUSE." (VIII, 512-13)

THIS IS NO SCHOLARLY TREATISE. Long ago I tired of the ivory tower. Homer never went there. He belonged on the wide oceans of experience, even as Shakespeare belonged in the streets. I got tired of the self-important bullshit, and all those attempts to compartmentalize, pigeon-hole, stereotype, and stylize. In my doctorate oral exam I was asked to cough up the critical attributes of "epic poetry in *The Odyssey.*" I resented being forced to dissect such a thing of beauty into a list of intellectual "characteristics" attached to a "degree."

At the time I was only dimly aware of the changes taking place inside me. Even as I was jumping through ridiculous hoops leading to the doctorate degree in English Literature, I was living the life of Homer. That is to say, I was in the process of becoming an Odysseus (the story a blind poet was telling to create himself). Even as I languished in the stifling classrooms of academia, I was adrift on the wine dark sea. I had already contended in the Trojan Wars of college athletics. Daily, I lusted at Circe's trough. I'd sailed to the Hades of divorce. I'd fathered Telemachus. As a grown man, I was contending with monsters that had little if anything to do with Ph.D. examinations.

Even then, ancient memories were pulling me back to the place where I was born, to the womb of the earth and the awesome secret of the marriage bed. Even then I had the faintest notion that there had to be some place of returning. As the years passed, the notion grew into a dead certainty. With the help of the gods and goddesses, I would finally come home.

Now, as my eyes close in sleep and the foam hisses in the wake of the tall ship with black sails, I begin to see what *The Odyssey* was all about. It was about the blind old man at the end of a life, singing for his bread, singing the old songs to evoke longings in the hearts of listeners, songs that stirred passion in his own heart for home. Even his name evokes ancient memories of home. "Home, house, abode, grave, native place, one's own place or country." "O.E., *ham*, O.S., *hem*, Du. *heem*, O.N., *heimr*, Goth. *haims.*" *Homer.* "Certain birds: Domestic, familiar, plain, simple."

Was Homer real? He was as real as Plato and Alexander, or you and me. And he suffered as much as any other man, perhaps more. He was one man, one life, one fate. Yet he carried the memory-legacy of millions of men from the beginning of human time. All those archetypes of how men finally made their way to Ithaka!

Poet, bard, skald, minstrel, *cantastorie,* Homer patched together a thousand memories into an unique bird-song about how men remember to get back home. Robert Fitzgerald characterized Homer as: "A living voice in the firelight or in the open air, a living presence bringing into life his great company of imagined persons, a master performer at his ease, touching the strings, disposing of many voices, many tones and tempos, tragedy, comedy, and glory, holding his auditors in the palm of his hand. . . ." If Homer, the living poet, was all this, how could he have also been the brave Odysseus, the man "skilled in all ways of contending," the "great tactician," the "master mariner and soldier" of whom he sang? There was only one way. The singer lived the life of his hero, in his psyche, mind, and imagination. He was, after all, an artist.

Poets lie. There can be no doubt about that. They catechize a dream into reality. Who is to say the dream is less real than "the real?" Certainly not artists. Do they, in fact, turn "the real" into dream? If you were to ask them, "Who is the real you?" they would tell you all about the truth of their lies, or about where their lies came from. With libations of honeyed wine they would pay homage to the Muse who sings them into existence and fills their sails as they journey homeward. They know that sooner or later they will surrender their bodies to her.

Anyone who remembers, lies. It did not happen exactly as we remember it. Yet we act upon it as though it were the truth. So the poet acts. The act is allowing oneself to be sung through. The song is only a memory, a made-up tune sung long ago by the Muse, the Source of all lies. The poet doesn't care. He's in love with her. He's willing to go all the way home with her. He'll put up with all her artful disguises, the ways in which she always hides herself behind beauty. He saw her rising naked in the dawn. That's why she blinded him, and why she made him sing about Odysseus. Her lies are virtual truth.

Is there no end to deception? Buddha claimed to have gone beyond the lies. That's all well and good for the Buddha. But not for the poet. The poet loves the song-mask as much as he loves nakedness. And now, from the perspective of the 21st century, I read the lies of this lying poet-singer named Homer. Bitter tears ooze through the flesh of my cage. My soul yearns to be free, like a captive bird, to believe in lies that tell the truth.

The human world seems out of control. Nations and people war against nations and people. Children kill other children with the weapons of their parents. Parents kill their children, and turn against each other. Terrorists plot the death of millions of innocents. Hot-headed boy soldiers seethe from anthills like Myrmidons. Men who call themselves honorable warriors brandish weapons of unimaginable destruction. The computer age has put a deadly weapon in the minds of untried children. Old age has become a curse, a disease, and people are forgetting how to get back home. All hands on deck are imperiled.

Lies, lies, all lies. Beneath the flow of disastrous illusion lies an even deeper truth (or is it all illusion)? Even if all hands are lost, Odysseus will survive. He will never lose his longing to fetch up on his home island. And the forces that oppose him are the same forces that have always opposed men and women—and by extension all beings. Will the poet find his way through the implacable forces of nature (and human nature) to the very essence of the song? And will that essence be one of love, motherhood, fatherhood, loneliness, hardship, tragedy, comedy, foolishness, death and regeneration? And will that song honor the Muse, the great Authoress of Sacred Lies?

The truth is, Odysseus will live forever—because the poet will live forever. It doesn't matter if the humans are all gone. It doesn't even matter if the Earth Herself should disappear. Homer is just a shred of Nature seeking to fulfill Herself throughout the universe, to live Her cycle of the seasons, to endure the drownings and the parchings, the times of plenty and starvation, the lying-times of peace and war. If Odysseus is yang longing for yin, then Nature is yin longing for Homer.

"I am Laerte's son, Odysseus." (IX, 20-22)

I AM MY FATHER'S SON. My father was his father's son. My father's father was his father's son. I am the "he" of a thousand thousand fathers. Thus, when I say I am "he," I am what my ancestral fathers have collectively made me. That is why, even if I do not always consider my father "sacred," I invoke his name when I tell you mine. It cannot be otherwise.

Because I am my father's son, I am the offspring of psychogenetic memory. The unique combination of remembrance that bears the name of Odysseus-Angry Man will do what it will do because the ancestors have decreed it. From ancient times they survived because they remembered how to live. Their power to determine a life is equalled only by the power of a life to determine itself. In the end, the objective is the same. Life is a jot, a tittle, and a going home. That is how my ancestors remember me. They must be remembering you in the same way.

Home is always associated with the land, the homeland, our home island, Ithaka—where my father and his father and his father's father were born and died. Most of us, including our ancestors, didn't get there without a good deal of effort. By the labor of our mother, and her mother's mother, we are brought into this world. And by the labor of our father's father, we are brought to our unfleshing in the great hall.

> "I come from Rover's Passage where my home is,
> and I'm King Allwoe's only son. My name
> is Quarrelman. . . . Oh, Father, I am He!
> Twenty years gone, and here I've come again
> to my own land!"

Arm in arm, we will walk once more to the old stone house. Athena will dress father in a new cloak, fill out his limbs again, put a "godlike bloom" on his skin. "Oh, Father," I will cry. "Surely one of the gods who are young forever has made you magnificent before my eyes!" Once again he will remember his youth, take up his shield and helm, and stand beside his son and his grandchildren in the forefront of the battle. Strength from the goddess will flow into him and he will let fly the first spear.

And what of my mother? I left her long ago. She died of grief, not knowing if I lived to fulfill her dreams for me. Ah mother, if you only knew. For every life I took, I forgave a life, and for every act of violence, I stayed my hand on my sword, and made love, not war. O, sacred bond! Is it not true that even though I left you long ago to find my own destiny, I am still one with you, and your mother Mazie, and your great grandmother Flint? Yet I have always been a source of anxiety to you, like a child who preferred to shake hands with the devil.

I know you worry about me. Every night, when I enter the underworld of sleep, you come to me, restless with angst, and "call out sorrowfully . . . Have you not gone at all to Ithaka? Have you not seen your lady in your hall?" Then you tell me you died because of "my loneliness for you, Odysseus." I try to act the brave man, but in my heart I cry in the darkness:

> "O mother, will you not stay, be still, here
> in my arms, may we not, in this place of Death. . .
> Hold one another, touch with love, and taste
> salt tears' relief, the twinge of welling tears?"

We all remember how to find our way home. If I listen, I remember too. The way home takes the form of the deepest longing—so deep that this present life is but a shadow of reality. Ithaka-desire is nothing less than the desire of all things to return to the land of our engendering.

"There is nothing meager about the soil," says grey-eyed Athena, "and the yield of grain is wondrous, and wine, too, with drenching rains and dewfall."

"MEN HOLD ME FORMIDABLE FOR GUILE IN PEACE AND WAR." (IX, 21-2)

I GREW UP IN A HOME GUARDED by the Ten Commandments. "Thou shalt not steal," "Thou shalt not bear false witness," and "Thou shalt not covet," were zealously enforced. I was soundly whipped for transgressing the Law. My parents did not want the Lord to see a cunning or deceitful son. They were not flattered when I took the toy belonging to the little girl down the street, or when I broke into the high school gym, or when I lied about stealing from the cookie jar, or when I returned the family car with beer stains on the front seat, or when I divorced my first Christian wife before a year was gone, or when I was jailed for opposing the President, or when I transported two tons of marijuana from Mexico in a Rent-A-Van. My mother wanted her oldest son to grow up to be an honorable Fundamentalist, and my father tried to be her strong right arm.

By and large I grew up in terror of the wrath of God, whose instruments of correction included parents and culture. The terror was compounded by guilt. Even when I was not apprehended for various acts of duplicity, I lived in the fear that I would, and more than once I blurted out the truth to escape the guilt-tortures of the damned. No way was I going to wind up in Hell!

Naturally, I secretly yearned to be free of the law. In this I was no different than most young men, or women. I wanted to do what I wanted to do, not what my family, culture, or God wanted me to do. I dreamed of the Trojan Wars. As I grew older, I grew more bold and daring. I began to trust my wits to keep me out of trouble. By the time I graduated from high school, I had acquired a closet-full of secrets unknown to anyone, certainly not to any "authority."

That shameful closet door finally fell open when I was finally ready to live my own life as an "adult." Even if I was only half-aware, I could see that those very actions condemned in the Ten Commandments were characteristic of my own behavior. But the fabled God Jehovah had not struck me down with a bolt of lightning. I had survived my childhood.

We are all liars, thieves, and covetors. And we have broken all kinds of ethical laws on our way to the crags of Ithaka. If you tell me you are not one of these I won't believe you. St. Paul was right about one thing: We have "all sinned and come short of the glory of God." And if there's anything I have learned to dislike in this life, it's someone telling me he or she is above blame by blaming me.

Not that I necessarily believe God him/herself is glorious and without guile—or that trickery and deceit are sins. Far from it. If God made us liars and thieves, then He did so because He had a certain predisposition for liars and thieves. It wasn't our trickery, but His. How can a perfect God make something so "imperfect" as a flower that entices insects to their death, or a coyote who tricks little cottontail into a trap, or a faithless male hummingbird who lures fertile females into heedless copulation? The lies go on and on. If God is perfect, why was He so obsessed with duplicity?

If God is also a liar and a thief, then why cannot Odysseus boast to the King of Phaeacians that he is a man formidable for guile in peace and war? At least he's "out front" about it. In so doing he joins hands with all those beings down through mythological history who lied and cheated and stole and carried on, with or without self-righteousness, who touched the sacred with the fingerprints of Hermes, Loki, Coyote, Falstaff, Felix Krüll, the Confidence Man, the Grifter, Raven, Br'er Rabbit, and all their kin.

I find myself in their company whether I will or not. Who knows how many times I resorted to guile to get my way? Am I proud of it? Maybe. Maybe not. Every once in a while I catch myself boasting foolishly about some nefarious exploit. Far better to admit it than to play the hypocrite, who lies like anybody else, who claims so righteously that he is not. Deliver me, deliver us, from our own hypocrisy. We are spiders who lure others into our webs and suck them of humanity. Yet we refuse to allow others to squash us, to say, "Thank god I am not like him."

If I too am an hypocrite, then let me lie and steal and trick my way into enlightenment. Let me sail with Odysseus, making myself up as I go—a hundred thousand men wrapped up in one ordinary, foolish, angry man going home.

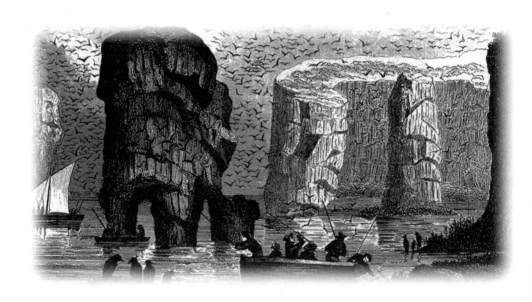

"Godsake, captain! Why bait the beast again? Let him alone!" (IX, 538)

When will we ever learn? Angry, bound for trouble, and to top it all off, boastful. Just when we have managed to get clear of present danger, we jump deeper into the shit. Even as we flee for our lives, we shake our puny fists at the quicksand into which we lured ourselves and our brothers. Do we humbly thank the gods for helping us escape the cavern of self-consuming anger? Not often. We yield once again to hubris. We let our anger flare and risk everybody's life all over again.

> "If ever mortal man inquire . . . tell him Odysseus, raider
> of cities, took your eye: Laertes' son, whose home's on Ithaka!"

And so the blinded monster who lives within us, mired and frustrated in the darkness of our own quicksand, throws down a piece of a mountain, and the backwash sucks us back in again. Only the fickle luck known only by fools saves us from drowning.

We may survive by the skin of our teeth, but the curse of karma has marked us forever. We never quite escape the tidal undertow. Henceforth, we are haunted by the doubt we shall ever see our home again. And if we do attain home, "far be that day, and dark the years between."

If ever there was a fool, it was me. How many years, how many wasted lives did it take for me to learn? Even today, crippled by years of habitually playing the fool, I am no stranger to the doldrums. Vainly I keep protesting, "I am Odysseus, raider of cities." You'd think that by now I'd know better, that after all those buffeting waves I'd be willing to admit, once and for all, that "My real name is Nobody."

The fool is known by his inability to realize who he actually is—and by all the ways he devises to camouflage his true life course. Without Coyote the Fool, there would be no curse. Without the curse, there would be no longing for home. Without the longing, there would be no death. Without death, there would be no hope.

The Paiutes tell a story about Coyote, who managed to talk a Deadfall Trap into letting go. But once he was free of Trap, he excoriated it and boasted of his own prowess.

Trap put a curse on him, and said, "I know you'll come back and see me some day."

"No way," said Coyote, who went away to live a life haunted by the curse. A hundred times he tried to blot out the "invitation" by defying death. A hundred times he remembered the curse again. Fool that he was, he finally went back to Trap, just to satisfy himself that the curse was not meant for him. He felt around tentatively with his paw. And in one stroke, Coyote went home.

Still, we do not like to be seen as the fool. We do heroic things to mask our true nature. We engage our karmic shadows with great distinction, summoning vast energies and enterprises, thrusting our swords and shooting our arrows and fighting our way into the open, only to discover that we left behind a river of blood and the foul stench of raped hearts.

Deadfall Trigger Trap will find us in the end. He doesn't even have to move an inch.

"TELL HIM ODYSSEUS, RAIDER OF CITIES, TOOK YOUR EYE." (IX, 551)

WE ARE ALL THIEVES, EVEN THOSE AMONG US who are scrupulously honest. We steal from each other and we steal from the earth. Every day we take something that doesn't belong to us—a thought, a feeling, a gesture, a glance, a word, a dream, a style, a piece of fruit in the supermarket. We uproot plants and trees, clear away weeds and swamps, take the lives and the habitats of wildlife. We swipe whatever we can, and not only to survive. From the time we were born, our ancestors were teaching us how to steal, how to get our way, how to have instead of not having. Why shouldn't we take it if it is there to take?

Odysseus was not adverse to sacking cities, appropriating material goods, ravaging women, and capturing slaves. In those days it was the accepted thing to do. You took slaves or were yourself enslaved—sometimes both. You ripped families apart to increase yourself. If you had enough slaves you became a king or a lord or an honored tenant. Then you could defend yourself against those who sought to enslave you.

Even today this is not an unfamiliar story. Most men might even acknowledge, at least to themselves, that they do whatever they can to increase themselves, to fasten down their holdings. Although it is not fashionable these days to enslave others, we continue to do so. We bend them to our wills; we imprison them with morality and values; we entice them into accepting the worst kinds of ideological slavery. Freedom is nothing more than an abstract ideal.

Slavery isn't even the worst kind of thievery. There are thieves who steal with murder and terror. Odysseus drilled a red hot stake into the giant's eye, so that he could escape with the sleekest and fattest of the sheep. Of course, the loss of an eye was a fitting reward for the Cyclops' nasty habit of seizing men against their will and gulping them down. Few quarrel with this kind of justice. Hammurabi's Principle. You steal from me so I steal from you. You torture me, I torture you. I take a life, you put me in the gas chamber. And so on. Not the best course, but the most gut-appealing one. An eye for an eye? Yes and no. No and yes. How do we draw the line? For Athena's sake, not with "the letter of the Law," but with the mind of the heart.

Good or evil? Who can say they truly know the difference? Certainly not those who call themselves sacred. Only those who have experienced both the sacred *and* the profane have any sense of where to draw the line.

Notwithstanding the cultural no-nos of thievery, we get a kind of charge from stealing from one another. Adrenaline gushes through our limbs. The sheer audacity of it takes our breath away, and the heart pounds with savage glee. By stealing or hurting someone, we put our mark on it, like the scar Odysseus left on the forehead of Polyphemos. "It wasn't Nobody." It was "I, Odysseus, who took your eye." And then we take off in our sneak-ships, loaded down with mutton.

"No way," I hear one of my dearest, gentlest friends protesting. "I am not one of those who takes things from others." Then I watch him devise a clever mouse trap. And I know—and surely he knows—that somewhere down the line, the mouse's relatives will leave their calling card in his sack of oatmeal.

"WORN OUT AND SICK AT HEART,
TASTING OUR GRIEF." (X, 159)

RARELY DO I MEET A GROWN MAN about whom I do not wonder what kind of life he has lived. When I have the opportunity to ask, I am astounded at his story. In so many ways it parallels our story. The archetypes are similar: the perilous journey, the absence from home, the encounter with Circe, the great storms at sea, the inwardly held ideal of the anima, the child (son or daughter), the wife, the monster, the goddess (god or Muse), and home.

Homer tells our story so well. Nearly twenty-five hundred years ago he was among the blindest of men. He set out to sea with fair winds, but it wasn't long before somebody (it could have been me) let the four winds out of the bag, and he was back to where he started. All he had was muscle, will and persistence through days, months, years of hard labor. And when he finally made landfall, it was to face the boulder-hurling armies of the Laistrogonians. How many of his shipmates did he stand by helplessly and watch go under? And then, having escaped horrible wars, he was cast ashore on the island of the Lust Witch:

> "We landed,
> to lie down in that place two days and nights,
> worn out and sick at heart, tasting our grief."

And for our pains, the Witch turned us into pigs. The poet in us barely escaped with our foreskins, only to face the Underworld, the Sirens, the whirlpool of Charybdis, and the agony of shipwreck. And when we finally made land again, only one of us was left. His name was "The Angry One."

We feel akin to you, Homer-Odysseus, we who were, and are, your shipmates. And we know you feel the same kinship with us. We are brothers all—enduring hardship, toil, and grief—all of us going home.

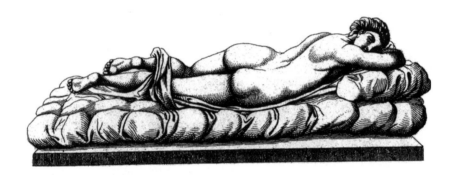

"Down in the sty and snore among the rest!" (X, 260)

Is there any magic more potent than lust? Neither men nor women are free from its power. I speak from a lifetime of experience, and so do two ex-wives and a host of lovers and one-night stands. We think we are in control of lust power. How foolish to think so! We call it "romance." We call it "love." But when all is said and done, it could be nothing more than romanticized piggishness.

I must resist the urge to be flippant. Lust is lust; and yet it is something more. It is so much more that it has taken me a lifetime to come to terms with it, to accept the lust-challenge in the form of children, two of whom were created by liaisons which, in the end, lasted no longer than a decade of passionate weather. How naive I was! What a silly hog! And yet I did not see myself as such when I was under the spell of Circe, certain that, unlike all the other pigs, I was truly "in love," and therefore not a pig at all, but an Adonis.

As young men, we are bountifully endowed with sexual energy. And even in old age our doctors usually tell us that we have enough testosterone. No doubt, down through the years we expressed much of this energy through the solitary fantasies of masturbation. But the fantasies kept trying to realize themselves in bodily reality, and every now and then we threw all caution to the winds and went for the trough like a starved animal, and it did not matter at the time whether the contents of our orgies were palatable or emetic. We were under the spell of Circe and her cousins, the Sirens. We had forgotten to lash ourselves to the mast. We were goners for sure.

But then one day, on the road to Circe's house, we met the "glittering god with the golden wand," Hermes, the errand boy of the Gods, who told us it was time to use our noodles, to look first before we leapt. And to emphasize his argument, he gave us a magic plant with a dark root and a milky flower. It bore a strong resemblance to, but was not, the genitals. We put those herbs between our legs and, wonder of wonders, we saw what Circe was up to. And we would have none of it. Well, not exactly. We'd have none of it until the Lust Witch had set our bodies free.

For me, that happened many years ago. And ever since I have not slept in Circe's "dangerous bed" unless she honored, beyond simple "sex," that dark root suspended between my legs. And when she could honor, not just my body and cock, but my dark root and milky flower, I could honor her. Only then was I truly able to "enter Circe's flawless bed of love," where she taught me that "mutual trust may come of play and love."

What makes a pig of a man? Is it his flashing erection and his witless pride in its use? Perhaps. Years of lust take their toll in jealousy and anger. No doubt appetite and passion are excellent ways to accumulate an insufferable karma. That which we try so hard to possess as "mine alone" has this inevitable tendency to boomerang on us, to bring us back to the consequences of our own idle fantasies. For lust breeds more lust, and is all too often blind to honor.

Now, as the days wind down to that single moment when I place my feet on the island of death, I am haunted by the hope that I will not be one of the suitors in the great hall, lusting after somebody else's wife. I do not want to be caught snoring among the rest.

"AND ALL THIS SHALL BE JUST AS I FORETELL."
(XI, 152)

ACCORDING TO THE MYTH, Tiresias was blind, like Homer. Mythical traditions differ as to the cause of his blindness.

One story goes that while he was hunting near his village, he came upon the goddess Athena bathing naked. The voyeur in him couldn't help but watch. For this transgression the virgin goddess blinded him —and then, in a fit of forgiveness, and because she loved the young man's mother, she "purged" his ears so that he could understand the language of birds, gave him a cornel-wood staff to guide him almost as well as if he could see, granted him the gift of prophecy, and allowed him a life seven generations long.

The other story says that Tiresias saw two snakes copulating on Mt. Selene in Acadia. He lashed out at them with a stick and killed the female. At once he was transformed into a woman who lived the life of a woman for seven years, during which time she/he became a famous harlot. Seven years later, he chanced to come upon the same pair of mating snakes. This time he killed the male, and became a man again.

When Hera and Zeus were arguing whether a man or a woman derived the greatest pleasure from sexual intercourse, they consulted Tiresias, who had lived the life of both sexes. Tiresias declared that a woman's pleasure was nine times greater than a man's. In frigid anger, Hera struck him blind for his impertinence. Unable to undo his wife's deed, Zeus conferred on the young man the gift of prophecy.

Tiresias' prophetic gifts are well-known. Among other events, he foretold the fall of Thebes, and revealed to Oedipus the murder of his father and the incestuous affair with his mother.

Circe sent Odysseus to the edge of the earth to consult the ghost of Tiresias, where he encountered "the old man with wrinkled dugs" (T.S. Eliot), still prophesying, and hungry for the blood of sacrifice.

One wonders why Circe love-witch would have sent the angry man all the way to hell to be told ahead of time by a blind shemale prophet that he would finally make landfall on his home island, overcome the suitors for Penelope's body, and die a good death far from the sea. No doubt she knew the power of woman in man (or man in woman) and could see that in the underworld, among the "unnumbered dead," gender differences were merged into one prophetic voice. Male, female, what's the difference when we come to the end? Does it matter whether women have more pleasure in erotic love then men? We are all reduced to worm-food, and all that remains are our ghosts, lingering at the lost borders of life, hungry for the attention and honor of the living.

What is the underworld? Where do we go when we die? Do we ghost-haunt the lives of those who continue to live on with voices of prophecy? Do we lust for the blood of those who died, only to join them when the time comes?

"MY LIFE RUNS ON THEN AS THE
GODS HAVE SPUN IT." (XI, 155)

HOW FAR CAN WE RUN BEFORE WE REALIZE our legs were given to us by the fates? How far can we sail before we understand that the planks rotting beneath us were milled by our own wilful destiny? There is no turning back, no changing of the course to suit whims or hopes. The way will be the way, no matter how freely we exercise our will. I can will myself to be in my bed tomorrow night. But I have no assurances that, in fact, tomorrow will come to pass.

Tiresias has just unfolded our future, event by event. Our hero shows no desire to alter events, even though there is much hardship ahead. At certain junctures (the straits of Scylla and Charybdis, the landfall on Thrinakia, and the cattle of Helios) there would seem to be opportunities to exercise free will—"if you do this with impeccability, you will minimize your losses"—but underneath it all lie the inexorable laws of survival. Angry man, if you are to make it home at all, you will have to exercise your will.

Not too many of us are allowed the chance to see ahead, all the way to the end. We welcome each new day with the same appreciation as blind-as-a-bat Homer, but we can never be quite sure what tomorrow brings. What appears safe today can blow up in our faces, like an irrigation pipe or a borrowed car. Our conditioned reflexes wear bat-blinders. We hear, and we think we know, but all the while the gods and goddesses are spinning out the real fabric of our days and ways. We eat mosquitos, and mosquitos eat us.

There is a kind of memory within us that already knows the future. All those sacred ancestors in our genes, all those ways of being blind to the reality of fate—yet millennia of divination have twisted a golden thread of truth. A deep knowing of the winding, crooked way lies within us all, and is most apparent when we descend into the labyrinth of Hades—when we must go to the country where no sun shines and no wind blows, and the only beings we can talk with are ghosts.

I know many men who walk a self-destructive path. I have no quarrel with them. Like me, they are blindly proceeding in the face of a self-chosen destiny. I cannot save their souls, for I am too busy saving mine. But I care for them, like a brother, and I want them to be able to accept their future, even as I hope to accept mine. I am no stranger to self-destructive behavior. I know by experience how often I ignored the danger signs along the path I traveled. And I thank my sacred ancestors for this knowing, for they taught me that I could still change—not necessarily the path—but how to travel it. They taught me in the darkness of desperation and uncaring despair.

We sail homeward in different ways. But we all depend on the same compass: navigation by memory.

We really do know. Everyday we awaken to the last sunrise of our life. Every night tomorrow comes. When we reach our home, we see what we already have seen, because we thought we didn't know.

"YOUR OWN KIND HEART AND COUNSEL, GENTLE ODYSSEUS, TOOK MY OWN LIFE AWAY." (XI, 227-8)

TO WHAT EXTENT DO WE DETERMINE THE FATE of our mothers? Or to what extent do our mothers determine our fate? These are not idle questions. As we grow older, watching our mothers age, we begin to understand how she attempted to determine our life path—and how her path was determined by us.

There is a curious and exceptionally powerful unconscious bond between mother and son. The prophets of modern psychoanalysis have made this quite clear. Freud considered this bond to be sexual, but surely it is more than that. In our childhood, mother is the goddess. We know no other. Without her nurturing we would die. In infancy, breast milk is the food of the gods. As we grow older, the life-sustaining stuff of her body becomes the every day world, maintained and defined by her. She is the milk-compass by which we steer.

Can it be that Mother is more important than Father? Even though Father may be present and active in the home, the dim memory of Mother's birth-body, especially in the early, formative years, pulls us to her again and again, like an unseen tide. When we are ill, we call for "Mother!" And we often look for wives who remind us of Mother.

On the other hand, our world is Mother's world. She gives herself to us in such a way as to maintain and define herself by us. We are the son-compass by which she steers. Even when she becomes a "working mother," as so many are in this modern world, she comes home to us, doubly sustaining us by her efforts in the work place and in the home. When we fuck up, typically in puberty, we hurt her, grieve her. "O what will become of my son?" she wonders, and tosses in her sleep.

Her efforts to correct us, to mold us into what she thinks best for us, do not go unnoticed. We are aware of her trials and tribulations on our behalf. We feel guilt and shame for our wayward ways. We vow to be better sons. But sooner or later, compelled to individuate from her, we hurt her again and again. Maybe we divorce the woman she chose for us. Maybe we get into drugs or alcohol or sex, or crime. Maybe we change our faith, or become atheists.

And all the time we are sorry for the troubles we have brought down upon her. Even the most violent and wayward among us tattoo our left arms with "Born for Trouble" and our right arms with "Mother." Even as we pain her, we enshrine her. We love her through a haze of perverted streets, and some of us even stop raping when reminded by our victim of our mother's love. We do not want to be among those, who, like Odysseus, was forced to listen to the truth of Eumaios' words:

> ". . . Pining for her son, her brilliant son,
> wore out her life."

How vast are the oceans between mother and son—but how quickly the son can reach her! Memory is a fickle thing. It can distance us and it can shrink us into the time/space of Now. Can it be that the borders of death are here, at this very moment? Are Now and Never one-and-the-same in the Underworld?

> "I bit my lip
> rising perplexed, with longing to embrace her,
> and tried three times, putting my arms around her,
> but she went sifting through my hands, impalpable
> as shadows are, and wavering like a dream."

"SOME THINGS A MAN MAY TELL, SOME HE SHOULD COVER UP." (XI, 516)

AGAMEMNON IS SPEAKING TO US FROM HELL. There's no reason now why he would want to sugar coat the truth. He knows. He returned from the Wars of Helen to an ambush in his dressing room. His beloved wife's lover sliced and diced his liver with an axe.

Without thinking, he had trusted her too much. How foolish he was, not to remember his own personal history with this woman. As the legend goes, he killed her husband just to ravish her (dubious) virginity. He'd sacrificed their eldest daughter Iphigenia just to catch a favorable wind. He'd stolen Achilles' concubine during the Trojan War, which almost lost the battle for the Greeks. When the battle was finally won, Cassandra, daughter of Priam, was "spoil" for his bed. When he landed on his home island to finally be united with his wife, he was still sleeping with (raping?) his mistress.

Surely Agamemnon knows, now that he has reached the Nether Regions, that Hell hath no fury. If you do that to your wife, you better not tell her when you're coming home.

Agamemnon's bitter comments about women mirror a typical male fear: because of what he has done to his woman, she will turn treacherous. Therefore he must not tell her anything that might put his own story about himself in jeopardy. There are good reasons why the fears of revengeful women should threaten the male psyche.

The fact is, men have hurt their women from the beginning of human time. Libraries have been written about their cruelty, their violence, brutishness, arrogance, unfaithfulness, and disregard for the most precious feminine intuitions. Agamemnon was no exception to the rule. Commander of 100 ships he might have been, but he was nothing more than a rutting, uncaring lout. He had real reasons to fear what his "beloved" might do to him if she caught him unguarded.

On the other hand, women have been known to be just as duplicitous with men. Take Helen, Clytamnestra's sister, daughter of Zeus and Leda the Swan. When her husband Menelaus was away (arranging a funeral for his grandfather), she slipped away to Troy with Paris, her beauty-boy, carrying with her a good deal of her husband's treasury as lust tribute. Her indecision about whether she wanted to return to her first husband precipitated a war in which thousands of noble men were killed, wives widowed, and children rendered fatherless. A woman with two husbands? How could this be? No wonder the old swineherd Eumaios was moved to exclaim to his master, gone for 20 years, "God curse the race of Helen and cut it down, that wrung the strength out of the knees of many!"

So the mighty Agamemnon was brought low, and so was his faithless wife, when she committed the act of premeditated murder. And in the dreary lands of Hades, Odysseus is counseled never to come clean with a woman, "never to tell her all you know."

What do you think about his advice? Someday we too will come to the gates of death. It could very well be that a woman will be at our side. Will she be holding our hand because we have told her everything? Or will she be hacking at us with a knife because we didn't tell her everything?

Let this be a warning. Love is how we want to die!

"NO LIFE ON EARTH CAN BE HID FROM
OUR DREAMING." (XII, 245-6)

TRULY, THERE IS AN INSEPARABLE LINK between lust for the body and lust for the Muse. I know a man who was in the state penitentiary for 18 years. He killed a policeman in a shootout when he was 17 years old. The Law sentenced him to fifty years, but there was something about him that softened the hearts of his guards. After ten years in solitary confinement, they gave him a typewriter. Since he did not have a table, he sat on the cold floor with the clever device between his knees—and began to write a novel. It was difficult, but not impossible. To summon the Muse, he only had to pull his cock from his pants and stroke it to erection. In this state of tantric tension, he typed on the novel, masturbating within an instant of ejaculation, holding back, continuing to type—over and over again, until his penis was raw as a hunk of beef. The novel was smuggled out of the prison and landed in the hands of lovers of literature. Ultimately, the novel gained him his freedom.

Can we blame Odysseus for wanting to hear, in the deepest secret of his soul, the song of the Sirens? The song is all about death, and if you hear it unprepared, you die because you are not worthy to listen. The song is also about mortality, and nothing is more mortal—and more beautiful—than the act of love:

> "Pleased by each purling note
> Like honey twining
> From her throat and my throat,
> Who lies a-pining?"

And what of the guards who watched him, making sure he didn't escape? They had no idea of the song to which he was listening. Having lashed him to the mast, they had stuffed their ears with wax.

"Sometimes I think this world
is one big prison yard.
Some of us are prisoners,
And some of us are guards."

– Bob Dylan

"WATCH THE DRIFT, OR WE FETCH UP IN THE SMOTHER, AND YOU DROWN US." (XII, 286-7)

As ODYSSEUS AND HIS SHIPMATES *RENDEZVOUS* with an inevitable confrontation with Scylla and Charybdis, the captain has special words for the steersman:

> "You at the tiller, listen and take in all
> that I say—the rudders are your duty; keep
> her out of the combers and the smoke; steer
> for that headland . . ."

The Fates know that no matter how skillfully the ship is handled, a half dozen will die. And if the ship founders, we will all die.

Don't imagine for an instant that you are not the man at the tiller. Our destiny depends on you. If this is a game your anger has led us into, then it is a deadly game, and some of us will not win. Our lives depend on the skill with which you navigate that invisible current pulling you from your course toward sucking disaster.

Shipmates! All of us are nothing but thoughtless fools, naive lovers, consummate magicians, and ready liars. We fight, rape, steal, glut, kill, create, build, love, wonder, and worship, and still we are no further beyond the reach of the wind in our sails than our dreams. We have sailed nigh unto hell itself, seeking a vision, and intimation of what lies ahead, but the god who rules the flow, the demon of the deep, splits our mast and shatters our keel. The cold salt sea rushes in and we are swallowed up by the smothering wave.

Let's not deceive ourselves into believing we are anyone but men. And though the gods come and go among us, our veins pulse with blood, not ichor. We die of cancer, pneumonia, consumption, jealousy, and fear. Every last miserable one of us dies. And every last miserable one of us is afraid—of potency, of impotency, of midnight, of the landing on Ithaka, of our own insignificance, of the charnel house of bones and ashes.

We do what we have to do. We go where we have to go. We compose symphonies and we plot genocide. We create children and then murder them. We build cities and then drop atomic bombs. We imagine gods and then set them free to damn us. We say we love our fellow man and then give him the power to tyrannize us. We walk blindly with our eyes open. We grope about and call the darkness evil. We rise in the morning and call the light good. We seek to know and are afraid of knowing.

You, with your hand on the tiller. Yes, you, "angry one." Where are you taking your world? What compass do you plot by? Into what winds do you hoist your sail? To what Ithaka, to what rendezvous with destiny do you steer? Do you care? Do you even give a damn? Are you so caught up, so ensnared, so oppressed by the mortal question mark of flesh and bones that you do not (or cannot) hear the wailing of your wife and children marooned on that miserable little island in the middle of nowhere? Are you so blinded by the lust for what you cannot see that you are unaware of the head boards giving way and the ship sinking into seas teeming with headless soldiers and poisonous snakes?

Let me look into your eyes. Are the pupils dilated? Let me see your hands. Are they scarred by nails? Let me touch your body. Is it real? Is there a gaping hole where your genitals should be? Let me hear your voice. Tell me your plan, your itinerary, your story, your Bible, your reason for being. Do you have one? In the name of all that is holy, do you know where you are going?

Meanwhile, the hour for landing on Ithaka draweth nigh. It is only twenty years, twenty days, twenty seconds away.

For years I studied the deadly ballcourt games of the Mayas and Aztecs. A former basketball player, I was intrigued by the "game as metaphor." And this particular game, requiring the combined skills of basketball and soccer, reminds me of the "game of life." While the Lords and Ladies of Death watched and wagered on the relative merits of the players, the little ball of destiny danced between the combatants. Unable to use their hands, fingers, or feet, only the most skillful players could sense the ball's direction. Only the luckiest and most capable could send it through the ring fastened high above.

Archaeologists and ethnologists are not sure whether the winners or the losers of the great ballcourt games were beheaded. Current research seems to indicate that the winners won the privilege of decapitation, and that the players vied with each other in order to attain immortality.

Times have changed. If such a game existed today, it would be the losers who died. The attainment of immortality would be a minor factor.

Do we play to win, so that the gods and goddesses of death reap us like ears of corn for their eternal digestion, or do they allow us to live another day? Do we play to lose, and thereby turn certain defeat into another day to be loved in this life? Surely we all know that whether we win or lose we will all come to the same end. Yet when death rears its grim visage above the horizon, we do our best to keep our little ship out of the "smother." Most of us want to live to play the game again—some of us even imagine that if we play the game well enough, we might never die.

From birth I have been gifted with a terminal lung disease. Not too long ago, I nodded off at the tiller. When I awoke, my life was caught in the smother. I'd taken my eye off the bouncing ball, fatuously believing I'd live forever. Death was looking me straight in the eye, and I realized, with great clarity, that I was not ready to admit my time had come.

I cannot tell you why Scylla did not pick me when she swooped down. I saw her out of the corner of my eye: twelve tentacles, six heads, triple rows of fangs. This combination of octopus and great white shark could have nailed me like a frog licks a fly. Instead I watched six of my shipmates disappear into her "horrid cleft."

When I look back at that moment, I am ashamed that I should have misjudged the drift—and astonished that the Lords and Ladies of Death should have decided to let me live another day.

Just two days ago, one of the finest nature photo journalists this world has ever known, a friend and resident of our deep valley, flew over the Wheeler Crest into the Bishop airport on a routine landing. His name was Galen Rowell, and his wife, as talented as he, was Barbara. The four passenger plane, piloted by a man well-qualified, came in too low, the wing crumpled, and the plane crashed in smothering fire. All hands were lost.

> "You at the tiller . . .
> the rudders are your duty; keep
> her out of the combers and the smoke; steer
> for that headland . . ."

I mourn for the passing of my brothers, who I loved as much as I loved life. They had played the game so well, many of them far better than I. Ever since, I have lived with the certainty that soon I will bring my ship to the rocky crags of home. Angry ones, are you ready?

"HE STOOD UP, RUBBED HIS EYES, GAZED AT HIS HOMELAND, AND SWORE, SLAPPING HIS THIGHS WITH BOTH HIS PALMS, THEN CRIED ALOUD: 'WHAT AM I IN FOR NOW?'" (XIII, 249-51)

RECENTLY I WENT ON A JOURNEY TO SAY GOODBYE to all my loved ones. I knew that within a year or two I would be gone. I wanted to say good-bye, to ask forgiveness and to forgive. My children and grandchildren and old friends treated me with affection and love as I drove from place to place like an old hippie, staying wherever I could find a bed and shelter and electrical outlets to power the machines that kept me alive.

In the state of Washington, while conferring with my oldest step-son, a medical doctor, I contracted a swamp virus that immediately invaded my lungs. At the time, I was over 1500 miles from home. I informed Meredith via telephone that I was not doing very well but that I was on my way. Several days later, after car failure in the Columbia Gorge in driving rain (Scylla) and icy roads in the Siskiyous (Charybdis), I arrived home, helpless and prostrate. All along the way I envisioned "home." I just wanted to be with my woman and our dog. Even when I despaired of ever completing the journey, when only an hour was left on my oxygen bottle, the memory of home persisted so strongly that there was no way—no way—I wouldn't make it. I would come home even if I died trying.

But I was not ready for what waited for me at home.

Penelope did not recognize me as the same man. She saw a familiar old beggar who needed immediate attention. Though she acted quickly to preserve my life, she had her own agenda, her own dreams, her own future, with or without me. As I looked into her face in the gloom, I realized that I had never seen such vitality and beauty in her, and never before did I feel so unworthy. She had flourished in my absence. Coming home didn't cure the disease that was haunting me, and for weeks I struggled on my own terms with the suitors who threatened to take me away from her forever. It was then I learned that there is a great difference between those who are life-warding and those who are death-warding.

Gentlemen! Those who vie with us for the love of our lives are not simply other men. They are the ghosts of our karma. We ourselves created them, with our genetic inheritance, with our waywardness, with our wars and our forays far from home, with our dalliances with the love-witch, and the drug-trances of Calypso. Penelope was never the perfect wife any more than we were the perfect husband. But if we are death-warding, we must lurk on the sidelines and watch as she descends the stairs in her slinky evening gown to stand, like a symbol of woman in her own right, before the lustful suitors we ourselves created by our absence.

Cynical as we might be about the behavior of our love while she (he) was absent, the challenge is worth taking up. When all is said and done, the dream endures, even as reality is worn away. It is a star that we follow, that we desire to possess, knowing that the light we see is a thousand thousand years old, knowing even that the star of our favorite memory may be dying or dead.

Nevertheless, we bask like sharks in the light of the star. We open the curtains and let her shine upon the bed into our naked souls. Though we may freeze to death in a distant light, we will tell ourselves that we are warm and cozy, that we have no need for masks or ravenous lies.

The forever-kind-of-love-road is narrow. It allows for only one. But we do not walk single-file, even when we are apart. We walk together as one. This is the great mystery of love. The cliffs are steep and craggy, and the trail always upward. Even as we try to break away, to go on as we have always gone on, alone in ourselves, trusting and misjudging our own sense of balance, she is in us, around us, ahead of us, going on alone in herself, trusting her steps, falling, picking herself up, even as we do. It's not that she dogs our footsteps—no way. But she is us; we are her. We wear one pair of boots.

Yet she is not we. And we are not her. We are alone on the trail and we don't know where she is. Climbing by another route perhaps. We call out to her, but do not hear the ironic echoes of her voice in ours, rebounding from the cliffs. A song surges into us like the wind. We want to sing it to her, to make it her song, not realizing we are singing with her voice. Not realizing that when we finally drop dead on the trail, she will drop dead with us. No longer will we walk alone together.

As you rendezvous with your destiny, ask yourself "What am I in for now?" If you are outraged that home is not what you thought it to be, you are doomed from the start. You have watched too many Hollywood movies. You will die like a leecher unable to count his blessings. You will succumb to the raucous laughter of the suitors. But if you consider the trump cards in your deck, you will remember who you are. The angry man who remembers will make his peace with his lover and with death.

> "Won't you, won't you give a man,
> Won't you give a man,
> Give a man a home?"
>
> – Blind Boys from Alabama

Home is never quite where we think it is. But it is exactly what we deserve.

Alternative scenario:

Pandemonium in the castle. Odysseus came home only to find that his woman was intrigued by the presence of the suitors. And meanwhile the owl called in the night and the shutters banged and breath came hard. There will be no slaughter tonight. The old dog will not recognize his master. The wastrel at the door is nothing but a beggar and his great bow is nothing more than a crooked walking stick. Throw a chair at the old asshole. There is no room as the table now and Telemachus has gone to bed.

Consider what is ahead. We must not shrink from our duty or our honor.

"WHY, EVERYONE HAS HEARD OF IT, THE NATIONS OVER ON THE DAWN SIDE, TOWARD THE SUN, AND WESTERNERS IN CLOUDY LANDS OF EVENING."
(XIII, 304-6)

MANY YEARS AGO, MEREDITH AND I WENT TO GREECE, looking for a home in which we could live for a year. We had this image of a perfect island, maybe somewhere in the Cyklades, where we would settle down and learn from a different way of life. But hopping from island to island in the Aegean Sea only gave us a pain in the ass. It was the height of the tourist season and wherever we went, tourists went. Towns were full; rooms were scarce. The beaches were littered with trash.

We decided not to associate with tourists. For three months we patiently searched Greece. But all the time we knew where we were really going. When we arrived on Ithaka, we knew without a shadow of a doubt that we had come home.

No doubt, Homer knew this island well, and loved it, for he wrote about it in accurate detail. Rocky little Ithaka. Goats and sheep and hogs and fishermen. A couple harbors, a few small bays, scattered little beaches, rock-strewn heights, olive trees, vineyards, occasional villages, and ports at Vathi, Stavros, and Kionion.

Of course, Ithaka is anywhere. You who live in the ghetto and trade your lives for heroin and speed on the street corner—you are not exempt from the harbors of home! Maybe you think the magical drug will get you there. Maybe you don't. All the time you are living in a little corner of hell, with a hard floor bed and no running water and a kitchen where cockroaches thrive, where four children and a wife scream for a better life.

I tell you, you are not far from Ithaka. Look around you. Ah, the rocky little island, the people, the olives, the fruit hanging heavy from the vine and branch, the modest bays, the perfect beaches, the tiny deep water port, and the stronghold of home. Ithaka is inside you. Never lose sight of where you are going.

Some academicians claim Odysseus never lived on Ithaka. They identify Cephallinia, a neighboring island, as his real home. They cite archeological evidence, concluding that no large fortress or castle ever existed on tiny Ithaka. Many times we toured verdant Cephallinia, camping along the shoreline, trying to get a feeling for Odysseus there. Nothing. Absolutely nothing. But when we returned to our home on Ithaka, Odysseus' ghost was everywhere—in the rocky heights, in the lush clefts and pockets of limestone soil, in the sunrises and sunsets, in the winds and rains.

Why, everybody has heard of Ithaka—the little island in the sea to which we finally come home! It may not look like much, and is nothing in comparison to magnificent Crete or Cephallinia, but it's home, where we hang our hats. We kick back and finally relax, putter around and drink beer and burp and shit and pee and sleep, and make love: where we make it beautiful. At least how we really want it to be. Where we are familiar with the foundation, the walls and roof, the rooms, the kitchens, the plumbing, the lighting, the heating, the air conditioning, the gardens. Where we can truly be who we are, even when we are not being who we'd like to be. Where someday we die. And if we should die somewhere else, our spirits will return to this rocky harbor in the sky-blue sea.

What if what we call home is hell? Then we must ask ourselves, Did I create this hell? Surely, hell is what we make of it. Like the "angry man," we must still try our best to get back, to come full circle, to finally say, "Indeed, I have come home." Will that day finally come to us? Believe what our fathers, the loved ones who have gone before, tell us. That day will come. That day will surely come. And when it does, it will come at dawn.

And if Penelope is actually a man, a lover, a husband-wife? What's the difference? Love is love and home is home.

"CONTEMPTIBLE YOU SHALL SEEM TO YOUR ENEMIES."
(XIII, 500-5)

THE GODDESS MEETS US WHEN WE FINALLY GET THERE. She is disguised as "a young shepherd, all delicately made." She welcomes us and declares: "They say the name of Ithaka has made its way even as far as Troy." We laugh in our hearts because we know this beautiful young man is the goddess herself. Her words strike us in the secret core of being. After all those years we want to cry and fall to our knees and kiss the ground. But she scares the shit out of us.

So we shift our shape. We answer, "Yes, I have heard of Ithaka, and somehow by chance I have brought an enormous fortune to these shores. I know not why." And we make up this incredible story about a man who has just returned from Troy and is on the run because he ambushed and killed one of the best cross-country runners in Crete who tried to steal "all I had fought and bled for." Afterwards, this fictional rogue sought asylum in a ship, intending to divide his plunder with his friends. But contrary winds took his shipmates hither and yon. By chance they landed last night on this strange island. They left him (with this huge treasure), and took off again for another port of call.

Why should we make up such a cockaminny story at a time like this? The virgin goddess stands before us, barely holding her shape. Though frightened, we can see clean through her disguise. But something portentous within us—is it the recognition that we are "of" her—causes us to maintain our role. Maybe we'll tell her a *kind* of truth, a *semblance* of the real story:

> "... not that he told the truth,
> but just as she did, held back what he knew,
> weighing within himself at every step
> what he made up to serve his turn."

The Goddess of Disguises laughs and hugs our tired shoulders. She knows how tricky we can be. She acknowledges us as one of her own: "You chameleon! Bottomless bag of tricks! Here in your own country would you not give your stratagems a rest, to stop spellbinding for an instant?" And then she delivers the *coup de grace*: "You play a part as if it were your own tough skin."

Athena is not at all adverse to acknowledging the truth of our relationship to her. "Two of a kind, we are, contrivers, both. Of all men now alive, you are the best in plots and story-telling." The best at shifting our shape. The best at turning every encounter to your advantage, even when we failed. Why do you keep denying who you are? Are you ashamed of your own magic? Do you really want to leave your destiny to the power-seeking sorcerers?

No doubt, the way in which we use our shape-shifting power makes all the difference. Those of us who seek to acquire the whole world as our home will never succeed. Too many corpses lurk in our treasure-trove. The souls of those we manipulated to our own advantage will haunt us, to remind us that we have not reached Ithaka. After all was said and done, we were too self-aggrandizing to shift our shape to Nobody. The lies we hid were too powerful to set free. We perished on the Island of Cyclops, in the Land of the Lotus Eaters, in Circe's pig pen.

There is no more compelling reason to become a master shape-shifter than to get back home. Death is nothing more than another shape-shift—a master stroke if we can pull it off. "Actors" we are—shape-shifters, who finally have to enact dying. Can we "play the part" of death" so well, "as if it were our own tough skin?"

In my own experience, truth has always been accompanied by falsehood, deceit, and a myriad of dimensions, all relative to the event, to the moment of enlightenment. In accordance with the focus of any event that has presented itself, I have had to act, to play the required part, to engage the challenge if only because I wasn't even sure who I actually was, let alone who they were. Those who kept demanding the truth from me only danced with my act, with who I was at the time, a person carefully weighing every step within himself, so that he could adjust his shape to the demands of the occasion.

Part of this deceit was sometimes marked by a seeming to be out of control. But behind the emotion and feeling there was an actor who critically watched himself playing the role. This actor was always trying to learn more about playing himself. And behind all this "appearance" was a man longing to reach the crags of Ithaka.

Never do we shift our shapes more often than when we know we are in the presence of the goddess. We want her to see how good we are at playing these roles. We want her to love us, even to lust after us. Nothing can be sweeter, more empowering, than to imagine the virginal woman-goddess consummating her love in our flesh. How else could we be able to take our ease with the sensual Circe and her promises of immortality? In the end, the actor knows better. Immortality as a pig? Never. We wanted to return as ourselves, as ordinary gods learning to play our parts well enough to make it home.

Soon I will awaken on the shores of Ithaka. I will appear as an old beggar, looking quite contemptible to my enemies. I will play my part as well as I can, for there is no other way to get to my woman, to my bed, and the hard oar-journey to death. Then, when I have lulled everyone into thinking that I am nothing more than an impertinent tramp, I will shift my shape once again. I will appear as I am, beside my son and my wife, and win back the only love I ever really cared about.

"Come aboard; share what we have, and welcome." (XV, 351)

RETURNING FROM HIS VISITS with Nestor and Menelaos, Telemachus, son of Odysseus, prepares to set sail for Ithaka. The most harrowing part of his passage to manhood is about to begin. He will face the ambush of the suitors (his father's karma). If he keeps a clear head, like his father, he will elude them and make landfall on the island of his birth. If he makes an adolescent mistake, he will become shark meat in the wine-dark sea.

As he pours red wine into the sand to ask the goddess for safe keeping, a young stranger named Theoklemenos approaches him and begs for "a plank aboard your ship," claiming he is being tracked by friends of a cousin he has killed and will surely be murdered if he cannot book immediate passage to sea. Without hesitation, in the extremity of his own fear, Telemachus invites him aboard, unaware that this is no ordinary stranger, but the son of Polypheides, a man "exalted by Apollo above all men for prophecy."

Later that night, having eluded the death-minded suitors in the dark passage of initiation, Telemachus moors the ship near the town and, having sent his mates back to their homes, ponders what to do with the stranger. At that moment, a sea owl (Athena) seizes a dove in the air above them, and the feathers flutter down. Immediately, the unknown stranger grips the hand of his benefactor and prophesies: "A god spoke in this bird sign . . . Your family will be in power forever."

"Be it so," replies Telemachus.

"Be it so" is an ancient truth, and it has been a part of the discourse of every holy saint. In fact most of us are almost sick of hearing it, quite convinced our lives are far too self-important, our ego-space too sacred to allow ourselves to be importuned by any casual stranger, especially one "in trouble with the law." Why, nowadays, Telemachus would have been guilty of aiding and abetting a murderer. We're looking at a dozen years in prison.

Yet the tradition persists. "Give of your time." "Give alms to the poor." "Pay attention to the beggar." "Entertain the stranger." "Go out of your way."

The bitter, powerful beauty of South Africa, forever epitomized by Nelson Mandela, names this ancestral kind of hospitality *abuntu*—variously interpreted and deeply mysterious—"What I give I receive." "I am because we are." "You are who you are because of us." "I help you and you help me. Be it so." "If you are offered help, you have to take at least a little piece of it."

If you or I or Telemachus respect this mystery, and we allow the stranger sanctuary with us, we become what the Buddhists call "Avatar," and the Christians "Good Samaritan." Because we only seek to learn from the unfolding mystery of fate, we open our hearts; "We entertain the angel unaware." And so we delay, for an absolutely important moment, our entry into Paradise. We honor the Angel instead.

And, if we watch with open eyes and feeling, the stranger will show us what is going to happen tomorrow.

"IN LATER DAYS A MAN CAN FIND A CHARM IN OLD ADVERSITY, EXILE AND PAIN." (XV, 487-890)

ODYSSEUS HAS BEEN DISGUISED BY ATHENA as an old beggar with a certain air of nobility. Eumaios, his "old master of the woodland," has taken the stranger in, slaughtered a fat pig, and regaled him with island wine.

As they sit around the fire, Odysseus angles for a blanket, telling still another fictitious story about being at the battle of Troy with the fabled Odysseus one bitterly cold night without cover to keep him warm. According to the beggar, "the great tactician" supplied him with a sleeping cloak. Eumaios, anxious to emulate his absent master, offers the stranger sheep skins and a blanket, and then ventures out into the chill autumn night with a sharpened sword and lance to sleep under a hollow rock, to guard the flock from dogs and thieves.

The next evening, Eumaios entreated the beggar to stay with him one more night. Odysseus' son was expected shortly and would want to hear news of his father from him. The beggar readily accepted the invitation and said,

> "Respite from pain
> you give me—and from homelessness. In life
> there's nothing worse than knocking about the world. . ."

Over meat and wine, they discussed the karma of the royal family of Ithaka, the death of Odysseus' mother, the now feeble father, the son, and then lay back to bullshit around the fire, as men are wont to do.

Eumaios:

> "These autumn nights are long,
> ample for story-telling and for sleep.
> You need not go to bed before the hour;
> sleeping from dusk to dawn's a dull affair . . .
> Here's a tight roof; we'll drink on, you and I,
> and ease our hearts of hardships we remember,
> sharing old times."

And so they drank and bullshitted through the late hours while the wind howled outside and the sleet dashed against the door—"easing" their "hearts of hardships . . . sharing old times."

As we age, we look for good stories. Not those happily-forever-after fairy tales of the young, but stories of adversity, crazy deeds, shining nymphs and lost lads, deaths, faiths and karmic conse-quences—stories that teach and ease our hearts, that convey the truth of light in darkness, darkness in light. As fall arrives with rain and chill, the prospect of winter grips us like a vise; the days grow short and the nights inter-minable. We look for ways to pass the hours, even if it is with a favorite story on the television, VCR, or cheer from a bottle. We let go of the hardships of the day in an easy chair, and seek regener-ation in laughter and remembrance.

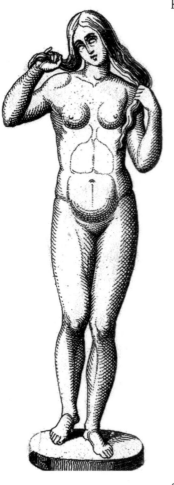

It is then that our own lives rush in upon us, for we are descend-ing the great mountain of our lives, and what lies below is the darkling plain upon which we ourselves have all-too-often grovelled, where in the darkness "ironic points of light" shine "wherever the just exchange their messages." (Auden)

And then, after the stories have faded into incoherence, restless sleep, dreams of searching, defeat, ruin, ambition, sacrifice, and rapture, the body cannot deny the fact that it has become worn and torn. We must arise from our sheepskins, for our pros-trates and bowels' sake, and shuffle to some place where we can let go a little more of the old flesh of this life.

"ONE OF THEM FOUND HER WASHING NEAR THE MOORING AND LAY WITH HER, MAKING SUCH LOVE TO HER AS WOMEN IN THEIR FRAILTY ARE CONFUSED BY, EVEN THE BEST OF THEM." (XV, 510-13)

AS THE FIRE RISES AND FALLS, old herdsman Eumaios tells his story: abduction at a tender age by his nurse, who was in love with a Phoenician sea-faring man, "handsome and highly skilled." Born of a royal family, the goatherd was too young and helpless to resist the romantic designs of his nanny, (herself abducted by Taphian pirates), who snatched him and joined her lover. The nanny died at sea, leaving the boy without father or mother. The pirates sold him to Laertes, Odysseus' father, who made Eumaios his Forester, master of herds and trees.

The old tracker's story is familiar to many men who acted according to their genital brain. I was one of those "sea-faring men." In the wake of my self important ship I left children, step-children, and many a lovely woman whose only fault was eagerness to give herself to my sweet talk. Ah, the memory of their perfect, pliant flesh hangs heavy in my memory! All those tender moments, all those open-mouthed kisses, all those thrustings and grindings and delectable sighs! All those times I approached the vagina-altar like a burglar, a confidence man, sweet-nothing my way into evanescent paradise!

". . . Making such love to her as women
in their frailty are confused by, even the best of them."

Even now, I imagine making love to nymphs in such a way as to make them cry with heavy-lidded delight. No doubt, this old man still knows how. But he cannot console himself with memories of fleshly conquests. Too much had been at stake when, as a vigorous man, he had no idea what he was doing. Such a wastrel he was, not to understand the implications of a woman's love. Even those maidens who said they wanted nothing more than a night of pleasure knew more than he did, for they held the secret of childbirth in their bodies, a mystery he couldn't touch, no matter how deep he went.

Who seduced whom? As I reach home, I cannot tell any more lies. I admit my complicity in this awesome act and its karmic consequences. A sweet-talking romeo, eh? Well, how many of my children were abducted, castaway, sold into slavery, slaughtered in the wars?

All I can say is what the old beggar Odysseus said, having heard Eumaios' autobiography:

> "But surely Zeus put good alongside ill:
> torn from your far home . . .
> And a good life you lead.
> Unlike my own, all spent in barren roaming
> From one country to the next, till now."

Two old men telling their stories to each other. Is Odysseus' story any more significant than Eumaios'? Surely not.

"NO GOD. WHY TAKE ME FOR A GOD? NO, NO, I AM THAT FATHER WHOM YOUR BOYHOOD LACKED AND SUFFERED PAIN FOR LACK OF. I AM HE." (XVI, 220-22)

MY FATHER, LAERTES, IS DYING. He lies in a hospital bed. Tubes sneaked into his veins and nostrils feed him with life-sustaining fluids and oxygen, and his eyes are misted over with drugs stronger than heroin. When he needs to pee, I pull the sheet aside and tenderly place his penis into the urinal. He can hardly hear what I'm saying to him, but the words gush from me like blood from an artery of seeking: "O Father, surely one of the gods who are young forever has made you magnificent before my eyes!"

He lies before me, a ghost of his former self. Yet I can still discern the robust man I knew as a child, the one who took me fishing and hiking in the High Sierra, who lay on the ground with my brother and I under the stars, and pulled aside the curtain of wonder to reveal the mysteries of gravity and astrophysics. I see him as he was then, and I see him as he is now, and I love him even more for all those years I rebelled, seeking my own way. Yes, dear Father. You are beautiful now, lying on your back in that nursing home bed, staring up at the stuccoed ceiling.

Beautiful? Do I not find myself looking into the mirror, ambivalent about what I see? The marks of aging are unmistakable. I who had fallen in love with, at least accepted, even exploited, my "best features," must now accept, despite all evidence to the contrary, that these wrinkles and sags given to me by a life of hard knocks are somehow beautiful. Beautiful because I see them in you, Father, and because I must accept them with the same ambivalence as you did—you who were the trail blazer, the pathfinder.

I too have come close to death. Now I know a little more about where you are. I'm beginning to realize that the fear of death is a deep river of quicksand that tugs at our souls from the moment we test our toe. I too have felt the fear and considered the challenge of letting go. Now I must somehow convey to you, Father, that I respect and honor the ways in which you kept on living your life for so many years after you were quite aware of the current that had grabbed you. Years ago you knew damn well that you were no longer able to hold on to the fig tree growing over Charybdis' abyss, that already you had let go to the sucking, swirling tides of death.

Who was it said, "Death ennobles us?" Birth does too. The closest I ever got to a god was when my god-father's sperm penetrated the membrane of my goddess-mother's egg and "I" began. I don't remember very well. Maybe the attempt to remember is a reason why I spent so much of my life trying unconsciously to make the same thing happen in the wombs of my lovers. When I was a child, my father was like a god when he came to my calls of distress. As I grew older, he became another kind of a god, a more malevolent one, like Poseidon, with whom I disguised my actions and speech in the hope he would not inundate me. As the years rolled past, he mostly disappeared from every day reality. I even tried to forget him, for I was living a life of which he did not approve.

But now I sit in your room, Father. As the machines drone and your lungs grab like feeble fingers at the fetid air, I realize how forever young you are. The intervening years passed in a flicker of firelight. You are still the boy tossing pennies in the streets of Goldfield, Nevada. And I am still the scrawny kid playing army in the vacant lots of Los Angeles. The withered hand I'm holding is plump and sly. It wants to dig me in the ribs and tell a joke.

Father, is it really you? Is it the same man who for twenty years I suffered the lack of? O Father! You must be some kind of god! After all those years and still alive, still breathing, still holding the golden thread. Your eyes roll over to me to look me squarely in the face, and say, "I love you. I forgive you for being gone so long. Your birth ennobled you!"

"GOD! WHAT EVIL WIND BLEW IN THIS PEST?"
(XVII, 586)

A BEGGAR APPEARS, JUST AS WE BEGIN TO FEAST in the great hall. We view him with a certain repugnance. This old fart has seen better days. His clothes are ragged and dirty; lice swarm in his scraggly beard. He approaches us with a story of misfortune in far-off lands: captivity, slavery, aimless wandering. "Can you spare a dime?" he whines, stumbling from table to table, disturbing our appetites.

What do we do with him? Do we throw him a piece of bread or a shred of meat? Do we throw a goat foot at him? Such questions confront us every day, we who are so absurdly proud of our possessions, of our clothes, our cars, our homes, our jobs, our beautiful women, our pretty bodies and handsome faces, our accomplishments, our life status. The beggar's plea embarrasses us, demanding that we come down from our lofty station and re-examine our relationship to the world around us, especially a certain knowing about what is ahead .

So the truth comes to us, disguised as something we despise. Or something we turn away from, truth so potent as to murder us at our dinner table. It is a dangerous, challenging moment, and rarely are we up to it.

Somebody said, "The truth is what you make of it." What do we make of the old beggar?

Walt Whitman said he gave something to every tramp who asked him. I try to emulate him, but what do I do when the beggar looks particularly sinister and I am walking down the sidewalk with my woman to see a special movie? I reach down into my pockets and find two quarters. Sure, I can give them to him, but I know it is not enough to bring him home to his own Ithaka.

I put the quarters in his outstretched palm, ignoring the three twenties in my wallet.

"Their hearts grew faint with lust."
(XVIII, 267)

MY WIFE PENELOPE HAS JUST COME DOWN to make her appearance in the great hall. All eyes are upon her. She—and the wealth and power she controls—is the reason these men are here, each one secretly hoping he will go to bed with her, and bind her body to him forever. But my wife will have none of them because she is not certain her man, her lover, her husband, is actually dead.

Among these men is our son, Telemachus. Of course he should be there, among those who worship her beauty and power. For twenty years this beautiful woman has been his mother. Now he sees her with different eyes, the eyes of an initiate into manhood. He has just hazarded the death passage in the wine dark *thallasa*, having just been in the presence of Helen, the crazy reason for his father's adventures. Returning unscathed to his home, he has just met his father, after all those years of longing, and he stands before his mother, no longer just as her son, but as a man.

I too am among the lusting suitors. Nobody but my son knows who I really am—a beggar in my own home, a ragged, dirty lout still smarting from the blows life has given me, disguised because I want to have a good look at this woman I left twenty years ago. Is she still as beautiful as she was when I left her? Does she remain constant? Others have told me of her faithfulness, but I can't quite believe them. I must see for myself.

At the moment she is speaking to our son, but in a manner unfamiliar to me. She seems to be seeing him not as her boy, but as a man somehow independent of his father and a champion of her right to make her own decisions.

Why, I do believe that if Telemachus were a knight, she would give him her garter, and gladly be his lady. For a moment I'm seized again by a fit of jealousy. I remember what I told her when I left for Troy so many years ago, in the event I didn't return: "Wait for the beard to darken our boy's cheek; then marry whom you will, and move away."

She is challenging that handsome young man, Telemachus, to take up her cause, for it has always been the policy of our family to be kind to beggars. She wants him to stand up to the suitors, who have been abusing her with jests, hurling chairs and food at the tramp's head, and, adding insult to injury, inciting him to fight another beggar, a despicable fellow with a mean mind and surely temper.

The fight only cemented my role among the suitors as a lusty beggar. Yes, there's some life left in the old asshole. I just allowed a bit of it to show. But what do I do about this beautiful woman who stands before me, her true man, and tells the suitors that the time has come for her to sleep with one of them? My very own woman—the women I thought was mine?

If love is a mystery, then I do not understand the opposite of love. But I am certain it is not hate. It could be blindness—that is, the incapacity to see, to really see, a loved one. God knows, I have been thus blinded. It could be impertinence, the kind of self-importance about one's common lot that makes one impatient with the slow growth of love. For love grows all gnarled like the olive tree, a few inches a year in dusty soil. Perhaps youth itself is the greatest enemy of love. When we are young we are blind to death, impatient with the few inches we grow. We accuse the rain for not raining or the sun for not shining. We find it difficult to grip down and adhere to the seed by which we were conceived.

As we grow, love grows. When there are blights and droughts, we grow stunted and inhibited; our fruit becomes perverse; we drop to the ground too early, or we ripen too late, and winter takes us. Perhaps we lose our desire for the sun. Perhaps we are barren. Perhaps we grow into ourselves like monstrous fistulas.

No loves are alike. Even so my love has grown from adequate roots into a fork, where it became confused and blind, impatient to know, groping through unfinished veins and labyrinths, but nourished by something so deep down, rich, and impossibly irrational that it could not but survive. My love grew houses and spun cocoons, explored tombs, and planted seedlings that glittered in the wind. Was it all for the hope of a star burning into carbon in some forgotten history? Ah, is love real or is love a dream? Is love the soul or is love the body? Is it love that distinguishes between the two or love that makes them one? Love is the opposite of love.

As I watch her descend the stairs, I am Eros. The uniqueness of her presence in the air, the way it kisses her, lingers on her, pants a little around her hair, sobs a little around her eyes, slithers around her hips. The way her knees bend when she walks. Her slight round-shoulderness, her frown of concentration. Her restlessness and ambiguity, the smell of lemons around her breasts, the hint of *barbarosica* in her cunt. The ways she speaks and spells, the geometry of her sleep, her breath in my ear. Her innocence, her seriousness, her treasury of laughter, the oracle of her womb, the issue of her weaving, the poetry of her silence, the *thallasa* of her eyes.

Shipmates! I am on a roll! It is the friendliness of her, the gentleness of her, the way she complements the meal, the way she finds those little, seemingly irrelevant things, the way she binds wounds, flutters in my attention like a snow moth, that burns in my gut like a hook on a line that reaches all the way to my corpse—that makes me want to sing the guitar to her, play the fire for her, buy her a horse and a river, tickle her ribs, rub her feet, tug at her whiskers, be her husband, father her children, and look for the rainbow in every room. It is loving the necessity of her, the reality of the gods' dream of her, the meaning of her why, the answer to her who, the soul of her good and sly intentions, her right to dream, her love of the stars, the rain, and warm fires. It is the myth and sex of her, the mother of life, the earth of death. It is the absense of her, the future of her, the inevitability of her death when I am born, the certainty of my death, when she is born.

How I want her now! I'm no different than all the other men, lusting after a beautiful woman forbidden to me because she does not see me as her man. My lagging loins stir and swell. How I ache for this woman! Now she's telling them that if they truly desire her, they will bring her precious gifts and act like gentlemen. She says she will give herself to the giver of the finest gift! How I long to tell her of my own treasure, stowed in the cave at Phorkys cove!

O woman! I have finally come home to you. I know now who I am. It took me twenty crazy years to remember. I am Laertes' son, Anger, and the father of our son. I am the precious gift!

"HE SHINES AROUND THE NOGGIN, LIKE A FLASHING LIGHT, HAVING NO HAIR AT ALL TO DIM HIS LUSTRE."
(XVIII, 438-40)

LOOK AT THIS OLD GUY GROVELLING ON THE FLOOR! You call him a man? No, he's an old man! He'd be lucky if his penis could reach backwards to look at his asshole. No mistaking the signs. He can't hide them any more. His belly is flabby; his breasts sag like an old woman's; his legs are getting skinny; his face is an old mango ravaged by insects, still hanging miraculously to the branch.

He pisses the hell out of the young men—but why? Is it that he still seems to be vying like a dirty old man for the mouth-watering Penelope? Because he has a ready wit and assured manner? Because he tells a damn good story? You'd think they wouldn't give another thought to the beggar in their midst. After all, beggars are a dime a dozen, especially among the wealthy. To all intents and purposes, the old man is something to be ignored. Who cares? Throw a turd at him.

The "malicious indifference" of the suitors is not the only disgrace the old guy has to face. The goddess herself is determined to abase him still more. After all those years of helping him, she chooses this moment to shove his face further into the sewer of old age accountability. The text is clear: "For Athena wished Odysseus mortified still more" (XVIII, 429-30).

What happens in the space of twenty years? We don't get any younger. Is anybody actually immune to the passage of twenty years? If I'm 30 years of age when I go off to war, and don't return for twenty years, isn't it true that I am at least fifty years old when my island comes into view? Am I absolutely certain of my physical ability to take possession of my "home?"

Don't ask me such questions. I am no different than you. We are brothers, and we face the ravages of aging even as we come home to the biggest battle of our lives. Once I was a kind of hero. Can I be a hero again, bald pate and all? Can I still emerge victoriously?

Is the outcome of this battle completely dependent on us? Even the goddess seems to be saying so. "You're on your own, old guy." All, of course, for our own good. But the very idea that our spirit lover actually *condones* our humiliation galls us. It's like being at the end of the rope and grabbing thin air. We can't even pay a pretty young whore enough to convince us we are not past our prime.

Of course we must depend on others to help us through the dark night! In the space of twenty years, "I" has become "we." If it hasn't, then we haven't made it home. Our children will stand with us, and our old friends, and, if we play our cards right and win a battle we are fated to lose, we will earn the lover who let us come in her, who always desired us with a dark passion.

Home: "a village, a cluster of houses, a particular house, a home-land." Only when we have learned to love do we come home. Yes, broth-ers, when we come home we lay jealousy aside. The bald guy who needs "a good knocking about the ears" has lived long enough to know what to do.

At first, we hide. We let everyone think of us what they will. In-stead of declaring ourselves, we "tend those flares and offer light to every-one." The suitors "cannot tire [us] out, even if they wish to drink till Dawn." The "old man" knows a hell of a lot more than they. Next, we let "our mind roam far ahead to what must be accomplished."

The name of an aging man is Patience. If you have not learned that, you probably don't deserve the name, "old man."

"A WEIGHT OF RUGS AND COVER? NOT FOR ME."
(XIX, 396)

ONE WONDERS WHY THE HUSBAND DECIDED to disguise himself when he came home. When I was younger, I was troubled by Odysseus' behavior at this point. It seemed to me that the most natural thing for the old soldier to do, after all those years of longing, was to reveal himself to his woman. Now I know better. But it took many years of hardship and sorrow before I could see with experienced eyes, and understand how important it is not to give in to self-indulgence when there is hard work to be done.

A rough bed outside my lady's chamber? That's enough for me now. Tomorrow I must go to war. Tonight I will gladly lie down on the hard ground.

Many years ago a man came to our School because he had lost his wife of twenty-three years. He was lower than low. When offered a sleeping pad he said he preferred to sleep on the hard stones. He explained that he'd fallen (temporarily) in love with a younger woman. Entranced with his dream of youth, he'd forgotten how transparent he'd become to his wife. She had a right to throw him out of the house.

All his adult life he had lived with women. He described his manhood as "domestic situations." Year after year he had worked every day to bring home the bacon from a white collar job. There were times when he wasn't sure he could go on. And he went on. There were times when he was completely entranced by the magical islands on which he had landed. All the time he kept trying to get home. Finally, at age 48, he was free to live on his own, without a wife or children.

He wanted to sleep on the hard ground. "Hard" symbolized all he had endured. I saw how green he was, how unaccustomed to bruises on his hips and back. "Are you sure?" I asked.

Oh, he was sure.

I don't know what became of this man. He stopped writing years ago. I like to think it was because he had found Penelope by spending countless nights under the open stars. And when he found her, he didn't jump into bed with her. He slept outside her bedroom on the hard ground.

And then again, maybe he didn't find Penelope. Maybe he lives alone, and still sleeps on the hard ground.

"LET IT BE AS PLAIN AS DAY: IF FIFTY BANDS OF MEN SURROUNDED US AND EVERY SWORD SANG FOR YOUR BLOOD, YOU COULD STILL MAKE OFF WITH THEIR COWS AND SHEEP." (XX, 54-56)

YOU CAN'T SLEEP? TOMORROW YOU FACE THE MONSTER and you aren't sure you have the stuff to vanquish it? What about all the other battles beyond tomorrow? Will the terror never cease? You toss and turn under cloying blankets. Over and over again you play future scenarios in your mind.

In WWII, one of my uncles landed on a Normandy beach—and lived. I was too young at the time to ask him how he got through that night before the landing, let alone the holocaust itself. He never talked about it afterward. I doubt he was the kind of man who would have called on the goddess, or even recognized her if she appeared to him. But he must have heard a message similar to that delivered by Athena. "Why so wakeful, most forlorn of men? Go to sleep. This all night vigil wearies the flesh. You'll come out soon enough on the other side of trouble."

This assurance—that we will survive the danger ahead—is the goddess in us. Many a nervous night this thought has brought me through hard nights of preparation. "Sleep now. All will be well. There will be an end to this." Naturally, I wonder about this way in which I trick myself into sleeping. I'm no superman. Sometimes my life is charmed; sometimes it is not. Can I really rest in the assurance that regardless of the odds I face, I will come off clean as a whistle?

A Marine three star general, veteran of the Pacific Theater, told me that before the landing on Iwo Jima he could not control his bladder. "Everybody talks about being courageous," he said. "But let me tell you, peeing in your pants is courageous."

Homer says the goddess came to Odysseus "out of the night sky . . . in a body like a woman . . . and stood over his head." She "chided" the hero for doubting. If, in fact, she was going to be with him, how could he possibly fail?

Can you believe it? Might as well believe, brother, and pee in your pants. There is no other way to go ahead.

"I AM AT HOME, FOR I AM HE." (XXI, 233)

ODYSSEUS HAS JUST LANDED ON HIS NATIVE ISLAND and made his way to his own home. He is disguised as a beggar. Telemachus and Eumaios the swineherd stand beside him as he faces the scoffing suitors and offers to test the great bow. The faithful old herdsman has just been asked by the old beggar (Odysseus) if he would stand beside this ragged stranger if, perchance, his long-lost master should suddenly appear. Eumaios replies, "Ah, let the master come! . . . Then judge what stuff is in me, and how I manage arms!"

Odysseus then reveals his true identity in a whisper: "I am home, for I am he." He does not say, "I am he, for I am home." He says he has finally come home because home is the most important objective, and that Odysseus is who he is because he was always trying to get there.

Exactly who is "he?" Ah, that is for you to say. Only you know—and perhaps the goddess knows even better than you. The angry man has finally come home. But the struggle is far from over. In fact, the biggest one is about to begin. "I am he" means so much more than "my name is Odysseus."

"I am he" means "I am home." We don't make such claims lightly.

If Death is home, then Death demands our all, and then some. The time will come when we will kick free of our self-righteous rags and face the ultimate conflict. Will the goddess stand at our side? When we say, "I am home," do we truly mean, "I am he?"

This is no idle question. Was Odysseus' imagination so ruled by the male myth of the heroic that he couldn't deal with reality—such as the fact that he was getting older and close to death? Did the old man think that his woman, who was almost as old as he, was as attractive as he? No doubt he was jealous big time, considering his bald pate and sagging jowls.

The myth said Odysseus is invincible. Reality said, Odysseus is an old fart. Gentlemen, place your bets.

"THEIR FEET DANCED FOR A LITTLE, BUT NOT LONG."
(XXII, 526)

MURDERING THE SUITORS IN COLD BLOOD? Perhaps they all deserved what they got. They had no right to profane the house of Odysseus and Penelope, even though their very presence in his house was the karmic result of Odysseus' own actions. Because they had lusted after her without conscience, they deserved to face the consequences of their own behavior. Thus it would seem that a fair fight took place in the great hall between the old man, his son, his goatherd, and the host of irreverent suitors. A man has the right to face his own karma, and to "make it good" in whatever ways he sees fit.

But what came after the "test of the bow," and the bloodbath of the suitors, has always puzzled, and in fact, pained me. Odysseus' old nursemaid, Eurykleia, found him in a

"shadowy hall full of dead men . . .
Spattered and caked with blood like a mountain lion
when he has gorged upon an ox, his kill . . ."

The faithful old woman was moved to exult over the scene. But Odysseus restrained her by saying,

"Rejoice inwardly.
No crowing aloud, old woman.
To glory over slain men is no piety."

As a man, I can at least partially understand the sated angry man's words. Make no public show of your gratitude. Don't indulge yourself in vain glory (like he himself had done with Cyclops.) The killing of men is terrible work at best, and if a goddess like Athena is helping you, it does not make you feel particularly holy.

But the tale does not end with the grisly death of male antagonists. Our hero singles out a dozen women who had slept with the suitors and condemns them to death!

> "Tell those women
> who were the suitors' harlots to come here . . .
> Take them outside, these women . . .
> And hack them with your sword blades till you cut
> the life out of them, and every thought of sweet
> Aphrodite under the rutting suitors,
> when they lay down in secret."

But first, he commands these doomed women to clean out the great hall, "to scrub off chairs and tables and rinse them down," to "carry out all the blood and mire." In response, the "sluts" came "in a bunch, all wailing, soft tears on their cheeks," and fell to work tugging the corpses of their lovers out of the great hall. Then, when the grisly work was done, Telemachus, slightly altering the behest of his father, strings them up one-by-one:

> "hung like doves
> or larks in [snares] triggered in a thicket,
> where the birds think to rest—a cruel nesting.
> So now in turn each woman thrust her head
> into a noose and swung, yanked high in air,
> to perish there most piteously.
> Their feet danced for a little, but not long."

I cannot see why these women deserved such a fate. Of course, they had slept with the men who lusted after Queen Penelope, but surely lust can be as sacred as any other human failing. Athena must have known how often Odysseus himself succumbed to the same human desire to fuck and leave!—seducing nymphs and girls.

Is Homer singing about the jealous sexuality of Odysseus, who thought that any woman who slept with one of his wife's potential lovers deserved humiliation and death? Is he singing about how important it is to wipe out all vestiges of a man's own guilt and complicity? Surely, Odysseus must have realized, after fifty years of life, that he himself deserved the same fate as Agamemnon. Where is the forgiveness, where is the compassion—and when does the bloody vendetta end?

The jealousy of a man can be a fearsome thing. It can not only obliterate the other man, but also the woman, or man, who has "slutted" her/himself to the romantic excitement of "the moment." Was Odysseus so jealous about his wife and home being desecrated by men (and women) that he was willing to snuff out the lives of innocent, naive, unthinking people, some of whom might have eventually become handmaidens to his wife?

I always come back to the true Odysseus, the man who would not only sacrifice his crewmen to certain death, but the man who murdered indiscriminately, without compassion, in order to repossess his wife, family, and home—the man who would order the death of women who slept with the enemy. The man who consoled his conscience with such rituals such as "cleansing":

> "Bring me
> brimstone and a brazier—medicinal
> fumes to purify my hall. Then tell
> Penelope to come and bring her maids . . .
>   Let me have the fire.
> The first thing is to purify this place."

Fire and brimstone? Surely, we men have evolved to such an extent that many of us are sickened by the excesses of our own jealous anger. Surely, we can see that the archetypal male myth has black holes in him, like holes in the lungs, like empty spaces in the cock, and that revenge must always be tempered by the compassion of the Buddha of Steady Breath.

"THERE, LEANING AGAINST A PILLAR, SAT THE MAN, AND NEVER LIFTED UP HIS EYES, BUT ONLY WAITED FOR WHAT HIS WIFE WOULD SAY WHEN SHE HAD SEEN HIM."
(XXIII, 101-3)

IT'S GOING TO TAKE TIME. I know it's going to take time. Even as I slide down this carpet of stars into the bed of sleep, I can almost see ahead to the denouement of this plot in which this Phaeacian ship plays such a significant part. I will disguise myself, so as to gain an advantage over the forces of darkness. When the right moment arrives, I will reveal who I am. Donning my finest disguise, I will become a really "angry man." Why, I've been building up to this moment for twenty years!

What I will do then is totally connected to my love for my mate. From the beginning I knew in my blood that I had mated for life. My absence has caused her great hardship. There was a time when I languished in the arms of Calypso like a little boy with his mother. Now I must reach into my bag of tricks, take command of my knees and bladder, and make my last stand against overwhelming odds. I must erase all the suitors from Penelope's present reality. All of them.

There are many kinds of murder. If it was feasible (and against ethical law) in Homer's time—that a man should resort to such violence to regain his true love—it is also true in our time. Men (and many women) have not changed. Underneath our veneer of respectability and all the different ways we hide our savage selves, most if not all of us are quite capable of murder and mayhem, whether it be on the physical, psychological, mental, or spiritual planes. Such atrocities should exist only in the blood and bone of men—not in our soul-lives, not in our memory, not in the day to day reality of living out the consequences of our deeds! But this is not the case.

We must all confess that there have been certain precipitous moments when we could have murdered rivals to our mate or our name/legacy. Instead, we turned to another path. We murdered them in our imaginations, with the arrows of self love and self-righteousness, and then became the very best of men for the sake of our children, our women, and our ancestral heritage. To a man we would all admit (with a certain glee?) that we could not have become that incredible man who vanquished the suitors if we had not come up from the bottom of the sea, like drowned rats granted a reprieve. We would not have been able to stand upright if we hadn't wandered around like simpletons for the last twenty years. And we would not be able to boldly say, "It is I, Odysseus, the Angry One. I am not dead. I am home. And I have come back to claim my own."

There is no need to talk about how I contended with everyone and everything standing in the way of my attainment of death. In the end, forced to be a wanderer from island to island on the wine-dark sea, I wanted a "forever" kind of love. Why? Because "I am home, for I am he." I am he who is home. I am a "homer."

Why else would a man accomplish the seemingly impossible and appalling, and then stand before his wife, in rags, with blood dripping like wrinkles from his hands and face, in front of *his woman*, his reason for living, his lover of a thousand nights of erotic pleasure—and fear, actually fear, that she would not *accept* him?

And then having to sit there, in the total honesty of our finest flawed poem, while she decides whether or not we are actually the real lover?

Telemachus, the son says, "Mother, do you feel nothing?"

She is silent, "deathly still in wonderment." Yes, the stranger looks like her husband, but for God's sake, he's nothing but blood and rags. Finally she says:

> "I cannot speak to him. I cannot question him.
> I cannot keep my eyes upon his face.
> If really he is Odysseus, truly home,
> beyond all doubt we two shall know each other
> better than you or anyone. There are
> secret signs we know, we two."

How could they have made love after that? A huge question loomed between them. Does the wife give one good damn for her husband's mythological bullshit? From the beginning all she wanted was for her lover to return. She was dreaming all those years of relationship, not his deering-do. So what if he returned covered with karmic blood? What's heroic about murder?

Hollywood has it all wrong. One wonders if they were finally able to make love when he returned. Perhaps they didn't. Soon after, Odysseus died. And Penelope? She lived long and had many lovers. Were any of them equal to the man who went off to war to defend the honor of his buddies Agamemnon and Menelaus? Were any of them equal to the man who had fucked, screwed, indulged his most sacred kinky lusts, with other goddesses, nymphs, witches, and bitches?

What matters most to a woman? What matters most to a man? Does tit for a tat equal love? Only the Guardian of the Death Threshold knows.

"WOMAN, BY HEAVEN YOU'VE STUNG ME NOW! WHO DARED TO MOVE MY BED?" (XXIII, 208-10)

THE SECRET OF THE BED—shared only by a man and his mate. What secret can be deeper than the secret of the bed? How many hours did we spend there? How many dreams did we dream? How many times did we turn to each other to seek that special hollow or bone? How many times did anger rage there? And how many times peace? My memory staggers under the weight of so much remembering!

If ever there was a symbol of the two of us together—it was that bed. In every dream of home that bed existed. Why, I built my entire house around it. "I lined up the stone walls, built the walls and roof, gave it a doorway and smooth fitting doors. Then I lopped off the silvery leaves and branches, hewed and shaped that stump from the roots up into a bedpost, drilled it, let it serve as model for the rest . . . And stretched a bed between" the branches, "a pliant web of oxhide thongs dyed crimson." To move my bed one would have to saw through the living bedposts of the tree and cut the thongs away.

Damn it, woman! I made that bed to last! If anything was going to live beyond you or me, it was that bed! Why do you stand there, you 40-year-old woman with breasts beginning to sag, protesting like a coy maiden, saying, "Strange man, if man you are . . . ." And then to tell the nurse to make up "the big bed *outside* the bed chamber my lord built with his own hands!" What does she take me for? Giving me permission to sleep *outside* my own bedroom? Why, that's like saying I can finally come home to my home and sleep outside my home. Big deal. I would rather sleep without you!

Was it Shakespeare who said, "And, seizing the swift logic of a woman, curse god and die?" But I know she is much deeper than that. She is testing me.

Would your wife test you if you had been gone for twenty years and slept with Calypso and Circe and lord knows who else? Indeed, you would be one of the more fortunate ones if she didn't bodily remove you from the house and tell you to start all over again. We better begin counting our blessings. Our woman simply wants us to sleep outside the bedroom—and she's even letting us have her blankets.

Yet this plan smacks of trickery. She is trying to trick me into revealing who I am—even though she already knows who I am, and this tries me to the breaking point. I didn't fight my way through twenty years of insanity just to play a game! But if it's a game she wants, then it's a game she'll get.

"There's our sign!" I cry, in a flash of anger. "I know no more. Could someone else's hand have sawn that trunk and dragged the frame away?" I would rather be really pissed that she won't let me sleep with her. But I can't do that. She has a right. Her right overwhelms mine. She knows she may very well be the one who holds my hand as I lie dying in that bed I made with my own hands.

I cannot but wonder at the miracle of this woman who runs to me, her "eyes brimming with tears." How deeply she has touched me, to the quick of every dream-fiber. Why did I ever leave her? What got into me? Glories of conquest and triumph in battle? What a great fool I have been. *I* am the one who must bow down and worship—not only the woman who waited for me and kept my affairs in order while I was gone —but the goddess who knew me so well, who contended with the chest-pounding gods to bring me home, to my one and only woman.

"Do not rage at me, Odysseus!" she murmurs breathlessly against my ear. "Here and now, what sign should be so clear as this of our own bed?"

The secret. My woman honors our secret!

"COMMAND YOURSELF. CALL OFF THIS BATTLE NOW."
(XXIV, 606)

IF WE HAVE ALREADY COME HOME, and won back our lands and our women and our children and our bedrooms, and have washed the banquet hall with "brimstone and cleansing fumes," and all our faithful friends have come to embrace us with kisses while we stood undone, "overcome by longing and tears"—why then should we continue to fight?

A better question might be, "Why are we still fighting ourselves?" The question haunts me as I finally fall asleep on the swaying deck of the Phaeacian ship with the tall black sails showing its heels to the swell. In my dream I am a king finally coming home to his woman and family. All is well—but for one significant exception. I have become addicted to violence. The wars have taken their toll on me. I cannot root the memories of killing and death and all the ways I have had to resort to force in order to uproot the "enemy," from my mind.

It is almost as though this antagonistic streak in me is actually like alcohol or adrenaline. And whenever the call came to arms, I stood ready. Even though I came through the worst kinds of carnage miraculously unscathed, I have not yet learned how to turn over and go back to sleep when the dawn call to meet the dragon echoes from the inscrutable caverns of karma. How will I ever escape the laws of eye for eye, tooth for tooth? If I kill the son, the father will come looking for me. If I kill the father, the son will come looking for me. If I murder both of them, the relatives will come looking for me. And if I murder the Cyclops, a god will come looking for me. The darker the violation, the greater the retribution.

Ah, this dream of life, so real, and so unreal! All at once the god of the universe drops a smoking thunderbolt to the ground on which we tremble. We bolt like a jackrabbit. When we look up, the goddess is standing in the scorched aftermath. She casts a "grey glance" at us and says, quietly, "Get a hold on yourself. No more violence . . ."

We can do it now or later, but finally we must yield. What we have done to ourselves and to others must eventually catch up with us and we must pay the price of breath. Far better to yield to the goddess now, to make peace, to go back to the Great Hall and proceed with the sacrifices, than to carry the souls of those we have murdered to our grave. Have we lost track of that which we truly sought? Was it to struggle and kill, or was it finally to come home to forgiveness from all we have transgressed?

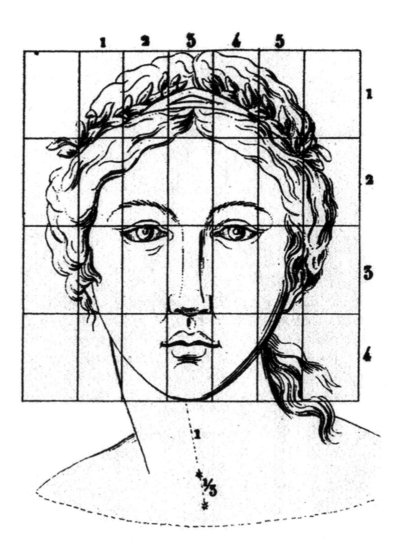

"Though still she kept the form and voice of Mentor." (XXIV, 613)

REMEMBER YOUR TEACHERS? I mean the ones who really taught you something. Indeed, they may not have been actual "teachers" from a professional standpoint. But whoever they were, they helped you earn your garlands. These teachers could be men or women or shemales. Gender doesn't matter.

The blind poet bares his spirit when he reminds us again how the goddess keeps assuming the forms of various teachers in order to teach us what we need to know if we are to make it home. "Look for the goddess," he tells us. She could be anywhere, in anyone. Never take her for granted. She is the feminine power of a man, his guiding light, and she likes to shift her shape to suit situation.

Every once in a great while, she will show herself in her true glory, but the circumstances must warrant it—a moment of great challenge, for example, when life is in the balance—or times of great joy, when lifelong objectives have been achieved. At such instants she becomes a complete ally.

But most of the time, she is in disguise, rarely appreciated, or recognized. I'm thinking of all those times I was given a leg-up by teachers who wounded my ego. Even Robert Fitzgerald, the translator of this version of *The Odyssey* told me not to write poetry, to give up my artistic aspirations. "Just get your Ph.D.," he said, and then proceeded to tell me about his own life. It was only much later in life that I realized how dearly I had treasured my teachers' advice, in many cases accepting/integrating the very wisdom my anger had sought to deny. It was the goddess herself who had appeared to me. I had been too self-engrossed to notice.

Many people spend their entire lives looking for booty, for gold and silver and precious lock boxes. Though they may not realize it, the shape-shifting goddess is the treasure they blindly seek. In the end, men realize the truth, when they have to leave their treasure behind—when they meet the goddess of the gates, the same feminine earth from whom they were born. They return to her body, that awesome mystical torso with its billions of disguises. But they are no longer distracted by these myriad forms of herself. They see only the goddess herself, beckoning.

To Homer and the people of his age, Athena was the name of the goddess. Although she was just one of the panoply of gods and goddesses, she was nevertheless a vast goddess, and she held sway among the people for a much longer time than Christianity's father god. Born from the head of her father, Zeus, and her mother, Metis ("thought"), she rapidly became the mentoress of men, a swayer of their minds, at the very time her father was deathly afraid he might give birth to a child who would be greater than he. His daughter maintained her chastity, and was sudden catastrophe to any man who chanced to see her naked. Yet she loved men, and followed them into battle, into commerce, into seafaring, into building and conserving, into fathering and parenting, and was even given to unabashed displays of affection to those she especially loved.

To see the real Athena, you were expected to give her her due—to recognize her protection, to pray for her good will, and to expect that, like all women, she might appear to you in full armor, with the dread *aegis* on her breast, holding up a shield painted with the Gorgon's head. On her shoulder the grey "sea-owl" would ride. Let us not try to interpret these symbols! It is quite impossible to imagine fucking Athena. She was beautiful, shrewd, powerful, secretly erotic, and totally beyond our reach. But how she loved to flirt!

In the end we have to admit that Athena is nothing more than another disguise of Mother Earth herself, who indeed has become greater (to all the species) than her apprehensive father. She is ideal Mother who teaches us through all her disguises. "Mentor" (from the Greek: *adviser*), a very old word, remaining unchanged from ancient times when it was first used in *The Odyssey*. Nature is Mentor. Look around you and tell me you are not, in this very moment, being taught by something or someone who is Mother Nature in disguise.

All our teachers, regardless of gender, are feminine. They love us; they are sacred to us; they are mysterious beyond understanding; and, mystery of mysteries, they often assume male form. Can it be that the goddess wants to be a cross-dresser, a male in drag? Consider the fate of the young gay man who was beaten horribly and strung up on barbed wire to die outside the city of Laramie, Wyoming. What a teacher he became!

AFTERWARD

"MY OWN HEART IS BROKEN FOR ODYSSEUS, THE MASTER MIND OF WAR, SO LONG A CASTAWAY UPON AN ISLAND IN THE RUNNING SEA." (I, 67-70)

BEFORE I EVER REACHED IT, THE NAME ITHAKA echoed down the corridors of my imagination. A symbol of fulfillment, even as Penelope was a symbol of feminine faithfulness and Odysseus a symbol of wandering, Ithaka was an ideal, an impossible dream of home. As time passed, the name underwent transformations, even as my own life contracted, and expanded. Ithaka became a symbol of death, Penelope a symbol of Maya, or illusion, and Odysseus, Everyman. For a time I entertained the notion that *The Odyssey* was an occult alchemical recipe for the perfected work: Odysseus, sulfer; Telemachus, quicksilver; Penelope, salt; and Ithaka, gold.

But then one day I set foot on the island, actually grasping the stones of Phorkys beach with my bare feet, and thereafter lived in Odysseus' mythical kingdom, breathing its air, eating the fruit of its trees and the flesh of its goats and sheep, drinking its wine, rubbing shoulders with its people. No longer was I able to entertain old notions. All my mytho-poetic bravura left me. I was emptied of all the conceptual garbage and scoured clean by the rasping sun, the smoking wave, the sting of banded hornets. I walked the island in a dazzle of frustration. I had not reached the end of the rainbow. I was not fulfilled. My work was not perfected. I was in the middle of the muddle, crowded by unfinished dreams and a fledgling love. I fought for a while, and then gave in to the pure, sensual march of days and ways, the passage of months, moons, and seasons. The myth was drowned in the daily demands of breath and the need to survive. I realized I had to transcend Odysseus the liar. The truth was more fabulous than invention. To imagine I was tired, or bored of this life, was merely to imagine.

The truth was that light bends and comes back on itself with a mouth blacker than night. The truth was that life hungers for life, and refuses to be satisfied with anything but death. Odysseus, you liar. How did you escape death?

I knew that I would leave Ithaka, that I would move on, that indeed it would be folly to fool myself into believing I had arrived anywhere. The wide sea beckoned, compelled me onward, as though I was a wave fated to spend myself on the rocks of some unknown coast, and I was powerless to resist drift and direction. Though it was within my power to hoist my sail into whatever wind prevailed, and to keep my death-grip on the tiller, I could not predict from which quarter the wind would blow.

The day of parting from Ithaka drew close. I stowed my gear on board and ran up the sail. The wind was from the west. I left the harbor and began a long course, beating to windward. Ithaka disappeared in the horizon of my wake, like a drowning star. I scanned the wine-dark sea for a blur, a smudge, a clue to where I might be going. Nothing. I was alone on the deep, and the sun was rising in the east. It was then I knew the meaning of Ithaka. It was the home I left behind.

The well of tears is always close, if we dig for it with memories. All we have to do is look back at our own lives—those strange coastlines on which we landed to take on water and provisions; those women, true and false, those who witched us, enslaved us, those for whom we went to war; those who wept over us, thinking we were lost forever, those siren songs and whirlpools of danger, those lies great and small, those shapeshifters, those deceptions, those births and deaths and doldrums . . . Those separations auspicious and inconsequential, those homecomings.

Are men born soldiers? Yes, and no. Though we have many ways of fighting the enemy without and within, in the end we must sue for peace. Only the inflexible and the senile continue to fight beyond their years of strife and foolishness. The old soldier in us knows how to grieve. The murder of innocent species/victims takes its toll. Little things can set us off—a chance remark, a thought, a sunrise or sunset. Few men want to die with curses on their heads. Those who forget about the curse enter a death-passage swarming with the maggots of remorse.

Even now, Athena is pleading the case of the angry man to almighty Zeus. She says her heart is broken for him. He was such a soldier, but now he is a piece of flotsam cast away on an island in the great stream of life and death. And my heart is broken too. I loved the man. The goddess within me loved the man. I wanted so badly to be like him, to come home like him, to fight the good fight like him, to make love to my woman on our marriage bed, to be reunited with my children, and then, at the very end of my life, to go off somewhere on a crazy quest to find someone who had never seen an oar—just like him.

More than anything else I wanted him to finish his life. To die into a destiny completely claimed by the angry man. To hear him say, through my own mouth, "This was my life. I would not take back a single jot or tittle. I have no regrets. I was no stranger to my own folly."

No longer am I afraid to claim my patroness, my benefactress, my spirit lover, my guide. When I get to the land where nobody has ever heard of me or the ship of my soul, I will surrender myself to her. She may not always have been kind to my shipmates, but she always cared for me. When all was lost, she found me. As I lie dying, she will take me by the hand. Her worn, soil-stained fingers will be quite mortal, and quite eternal. In this life her name will be the name of my wife. In death, her name will shape-shift to Athena, goddess, body, *thallasa*, earth, universe.

I will embark on my journey to the land that has never seen an oar—a desert land of little rain. In this land I will surrender the rudder, the oar, and the sail to the Furies who were so hungry for the consequences of my deeds. They will sit at the table of my life and consume every morsel.

No need to speak of the end, not yet. I am still marooned on Calypso's Isle of Illusion, and my woman's heart is "broken" for me, "so long a castaway. . . in the running sea."

Steven Foster, wise elder, trickster, wilderness guide, brilliant student of nature, beloved mentor, whole-hearted friend to thousands, and broken-hearted voyager, unravels the archetypal journey of Odysseus, seeking the roots of the contemporary man's struggles and joys, roots that reach across time and anchor Everyman's journey in a matrix of longing and lament. *Bound for the Crags of Ithaka* is an enchanted and poetic meditation on one of the foundational myths of the western world. A man of letters, Steven has wandered intimately through the wilderseas and the islands of Ithaka and has lived high-seas adventures and crises every one of his days for over 40 years.

– Bill Plotkin, Director, Animas Valley Institute, author of *Soulcraft*

Fortunate is the man who knows he is dying. He can take time to remember the story of his life with all its adventure, treachery, and beauty. He can choose to forgive those who have betrayed him and ask forgiveness of those he has betrayed, laying down the burdens of resentment too heavy to carry out of this world. He can finally receive the gift of feeling the deep mystery of the one life that has been his and finally receive the grace of self-acceptance. In his *Bound for the Crags of Ithaka*, Steven Foster has shown us how to find our story in the archetypal tale of Odysseus as he reflects on his own journey as Wanderer, Hero, Lover, Warrior, and Fool.

– Wesley Burwell, D. Min, Diplomate, American Association of Pastoral Counselors; Spiritual Care Coordinator, Seacoast Hospice, Exeter, NH

I have just finished your book. I gobbled it up. It is a wonderful book. As my beloved second son, who has wisdom and gentleness way beyond his years, gets ready to leave home, I want to give it to him (make him read it) so he can understand a little more what the hell he's gotten himself into.

– Joseph Woolley, Ph.D., Director, Drug Metabolism and Pharmacokinetics Research and Development, GlaxoSmithKline

As with everything Steven writes, there is a profound calling here. Will you heed the call or forever wonder if your ship was worthy of the journey to Ithaka? If you do feel the call of mystery and adventure on the mythic journey home to your true nature, then please, please cross this beautiful bridge. Coyote is darting across that bridge for the final time now and his words, as always, are like petals tossed to the four winds. Read, drink, and celebrate the many ways these petals land in the place called your life.

– Jed Swift, Director, Department of Ecopsychology, Naropa University

As a long-time vision quest guide, taking people on journeys to a mythical underworld and back, Steven Foster now offers us a guide for the ultimate journey: to life's end and beyond. Read the wise words contained in this book, knowing that you too must one day navigate your own great passage home. "[Then] I knew," Steven writes, "that dying to live and living to die were one and the same." With his help, may you too know this to be true.

– Scott Eberle, M.D., Director, Hospice Center for Wellness in Medicine, Sonoma County, CA

I felt enormous respect for the scribing of a hard, grand story, almost too big for the telling. You have created an incredible piece of work that is life review at its best—healing, not just for you, but in and for humanities past and future, now connected through your journey. Can anything else much matter (this is a real question)? What a gift of your blood, sweat, and precious breath, to all of us sharing the same journey, the same crags, just shape-shifted in our own worlds.

– Bruce Kelly, M.D., Director, Hospice of Asheville, N.C.

Like all of Foster's books, *Bound for the Crags of Ithaka* takes us on the mythic journey that is the ordinary struggle men face each day of their lives. Pain, fear, war, anger, betrayal, lust, intimacy . . . Are "windows on our souls, yearnings . . . If we fall asleep too long, we perish. It is about the uncertain, "great art . . . of living and dying. The path home, the place where the heart and soul are free to thrive in Ithaka, is delicious. Taste it.

> – Jeffrey Duvall, Vision Fast Midwife, author of *Men, Meaning and Prayer*

Lyrical and elegant prose that is about falling, getting back up, redemption, glory and grace. I can honestly say I've never read anything quite like Steven Foster's song of real events, of real men, humanized, mythologized, and filtered through hundreds of years of fireside telling. A must read for anyone who is looking for home. . .

> – John Lee, author of *The Flying Boy* and *At My Father's Wedding*

If you have read any of Steven Foster's previous writing, I'll tell you that you are in for a rich meal of the sort that you already know. If this is the first time you've encountered his work, I'll say that you have a deep and fascinating experience ahead. What he's done here is to take the great, original Western narrative (Homer's *Odyssey*) and used it as a guide and companion to his own journey through the second half of his life. Reading it, you'll wonder at all that you didn't think of (and your teacher didn't understand) when you read excerpts from Homer in college. And you'll see how ancient myths can come back to full life in the hands of a wise contemporary.

> – William Bridges, Leading consultant on life transitions with Pac Bell, Kaiser Permanente, Intel, Proctor and Gamble, Hewlett-Packard, McDonnell Douglas; author of *Transitions*